Raising a Catholic Family

Today

Building a Domestic Church

A Handbook for Parents

John Bosio

NIHIL OBSTAT
Rev. Andrew J. Bulso, S.T.L.
Censor Librorum

IMPRIMATUR
+Most Rev. J. Mark Spalding, D.D., J.C.L.
Bishop of Nashville
Diocese of Nashville
Date: October 14, 2022

For bulk discount purchases, please inquire at: Jbosio1@aol.com

ISBN: 978-0-578-38880-9
Publisher: JohnBosio

DEDICATION

To my parents and grandparents,
my extended family,
the circle of friends and neighbors,
teachers, priests, and nuns,
who were part of the village
that formed me as a child.

ACKNOWLEDGEMENTS

I want to express my appreciation to Parnell Donahue, M.D., pediatrician and author of parenting books, for reading the manuscript, making suggestions, and sharing his extensive experience about families. I also want to recognize all the friends who encouraged me in this project, and provided valuable feedback to the first drafts of this book, among these are: Danielle Bean, Author, Speaker and Podcaster; Rebecca Czarka, Songwriter and Artist; Rebecca Hammel Ph.D., Superintendent of Catholic Schools - Diocese of Nashville; Eileen Ponder M.Div., Executive Director, Ministry Resources - Ave Maria Press; Lauri Przybysz Ph.D., National Institute for the Family - Executive Team; David Thomas Ph.D., Theologian; Socorro Truchan MA, Associate Director Parish Life and Lay Leadership, Domestic Church – Diocese of Kalamazoo; and Susan Vogt MA, Speaker and Award-Winning Author.

I am fortunate to have such good friends.

TABLE OF CONTENTS

INTRODUCTION 1

BE INTENTIONAL 1
MAKE ROOM FOR JESUS IN YOUR HOME 4
THE PLAN 5
A WORD OF HOPE 7
WHO IS THE BOOK FOR? 7
HOW TO USE THIS BOOK 8
WHAT THIS BOOK IS NOT 9
   Suggestion: 10
   Home Blessing 11
   Track Your Family's Journey 12

HOME IS OUR SANCTUARY 13

HOME 13
OUR HOME IS OUR HAVEN 14
HOME IS WHERE CHILDREN NEED TO FEEL SAFE 15
MANAGING CONFLICTS 16
THERE IS HELP 20
ANOTHER ASPECT OF SAFETY – SETTING BOUNDARIES 21
   Action: 23
   Suggestions: 23
   Conversation Starters for Families 24
   Conversation Starters for Parents or Groups 25
   A Parent's Prayer 26

HOME IS WHERE LOVE RESIDES 27

SACRED SPACES 27
YOUR HOME IS A SACRED SPACE 28
MY EXPERIENCE OF HOME 30
HOME IS WHERE WE ARE TOUCHED BY LOVE 32
YOUR HOME IS GOD'S WORKSHOP 34
THE SACRAMENTS GIVE US A SPECIAL RELATIONSHIP WITH THE TRINITY 35
HUSBAND AND WIFE, AN ICON OF GOD'S LOVE 37
LOVE DWELLS IN THE SINGLE PARENT'S HOME 38
   Action: 40
   Suggestions: 40
   Conversation Starters for Families 41
   Conversation Starters for Parents or Groups 42

HOME IS A SCHOOL OF PRAYER 43

A FATHER'S BLESSING 43
YOUR HOME IS A DOMESTIC CHURCH 45

YOUR HOME IS A CRADLE OF THE CHURCH 46

YOUR HOME IS THE FIRST PLACE OF WORSHIP 47

PRAYER RITUALS OF THE CATHOLIC HOME 48

SACRAMENTALS—TOOLS FOR PRAYER 51

WE ARE NOT ALONE 52

PRAYING WITH THE COMMUNION OF SAINTS 55

    Action: *57*

    Suggestions: *57*

    Conversation Starters for Families *58*

    Conversation Starters for Parents or Groups *59*

HOME IS AN APPRENTICESHIP TO LOVING **60**

LOVE 60

THE IMPORTANCE OF GOOD HABITS 62

LOVE RITUALS 63

LOVE RITUALS ARE NECESSARY TO KEEP THE FAMILY STRONG 66

THE RITUALS OF THE UNIVERSAL CHURCH ARE A BLUEPRINT FOR THE RITUALS OF THE
CATHOLIC HOME 67

    Examples of love rituals that connect and create communion *71*

    Examples of love rituals through which we forgive and help one another heal *73*

    Examples of love rituals through which we serve one another. *75*

IN THE SACRAMENTS CHRIST FEEDS OUR LOVE 76

SEVEN DAILY LOVE RITUALS FOR COUPLES 77

    Action: *78*

    Suggestions: *78*

    Conversation Starters for Families *79*

    Conversation Starters for Parents or Groups *80*

HOME IS WHERE WE LEARN TO LIVE IN GOD'S TIME **81**

EACH DAY IS A WONDERFUL GIFT FROM GOD 81

A LESSON LEARNED 83

IT'S GOD'S TIME 84

GOD'S TIME HAS NO BOUNDARIES 86

TIME IN THE LIFE OF THE CHURCH 88

SUNDAYS – CELEBRATING THE LORD'S DAY 89

FRIDAYS – DAYS OF PENANCE 90

THE LITURGICAL SEASONS 91

THE ADVENT SEASON 91

THE CHRISTMAS SEASON 92

ORDINARY TIME, PART 1, ... 92

THE LENTEN SEASON 92

THE EASTER TRIDUUM 93

THE EASTER SEASON 94

ORDINARY TIME, PART 2, ... 94

CELEBRATE YOUR FAMILY'S SPIRITUAL MILESTONES 95

Action: 97

Suggestions: 97

Conversation Starters for Families 98

Conversation Starters for Parents or Groups 99

HOME IS A TRAINING CAMP FOR DISCIPLESHIP 100

TRAINING CAMP 100

THE POWER OF OUR EXAMPLE 102

PASSING ON THE FAITH 104

COACHING YOUR CHILDREN 106

YOUR HOME IS SACRED GROUND 107

"IT TAKES A VILLAGE" 108

GODPARENTS AND GRANDPARENTS 110

THE PARISH COMMUNITY 113

YOUR LOVE AND YOUR FAITH WILL RADIATE FROM YOUR HOME 115

Action: 116

Suggestions: 116

Conversation Starters for Families 117

Conversation Starters for Parents or Groups 118

CONCLUSION 119

THE ROLE OF THE PARENT 119

Reflection: 119

APPENDIX 120

BASIC CATHOLIC PRAYERS 120

The Sign of the Cross 120

The Our Father 120

The Hail Mary 120

The Glory Be 121

The Morning Offering 121

Prayer to the Guardian Angel 121

Grace Before Meals 121

Act of Contrition 122

Prayer to St. Joseph 122

Prayer to Saint Michael the Archangel 122

Family Blessing at Bedtime 123

Memorare 123

Prayer to the Holy Family 124

AUTHOR 125

BOOKS BY THE AUTHOR 126

LIST OF ABBREVIATIONS

AL	Amoris Laetitia *(The Joy of Love)* – Pope Francis
CARA	Center for Applied Research in the Apostolate
CCC	Catechism of the Catholic Church
DCE	Deus Caritas Est – Pope Benedict XVI
EG	Evangelii Gaudium *(The Joy of the Gospel)* – Pope Francis
EN	Evangelii Nuntiandi *(In Proclaiming the Gospel)* – Pope Paul VI
FC	Familiaris Consortio *(On the Family)* – Pope John Paul II
GS	Gaudium at Spes *(Joy and Hope)* – Second Vatican Council
LL	Marriage: Love and Life in the Divine Plan - USCCB

"Parents must learn to form their family as a 'domestic church,' a church of the home as it were, where God is honored, his law is respected, prayer is a normal event, virtue is transmitted by word and example, and everyone shares the hopes, the problems, and suffering of everyone else."

St. John Paul II

(Homily at Aqueduct Racetrack, Brooklyn, New York, October 6, 1995)

INTRODUCTION

Be Intentional

It was 4:00 on a Wednesday afternoon. A gentle knock at the door of my office caught my attention. "Come in!" I said. An elderly lady appeared at the entrance, walking slowly, and leaning on a cane. I got up to meet her. She stopped. "Sir, can I speak to you?"

"Sure! Sit down, please," I replied, pointing to a chair.

The woman introduced herself as Maggie and explained, "I just dropped off two students attending your religious education program." I was the director of the religious education programs at the parish where we met. With a smile, she continued, "You probably know 'them-boys' because they have a tendency to get into trouble." I nodded. I knew who she was talking about. Paul was in the second grade, and Jack was in the fourth. She continued, "I don't know if you are aware of this, but both of their parents are in jail. I am their grandmother, and I take care of them. My husband passed. I feel very strongly about making sure that they are raised Catholic."

She paused to take a breath and then continued, "When my daughter had these children baptized, she promised that she would raise them Catholic. She is not here right now, so I am fulfilling her responsibility. I want them to grow up knowing the difference between right and wrong and to develop habits that will serve them well in life. Faith in God and the practice of the sacraments have been a good guide and the source of strength for me throughout my life. I want the same for them."

"So, you bring them to religious education classes. What else do you do to raise them Catholic?" I asked. "I take them to Mass every Sunday. We pray together at home. I read bible stories and stories about the saints. And that is why I came to see you today. Do you have any simple books on the lives of the saints I can borrow?"

"Yes, of course!" I replied.

"What else do you do to pass on your faith?" I asked.

Maggie continued, "I tell them that God is with them all the time, and they can turn to him for help. And, of course, I pay close attention to the friends they associate with and what they learn in public school."

We spoke for almost an hour.

This exchange happened over 50 years ago, a time when raising a Catholic family for a single grandmother required significant effort. Today, unfortunately, her task would be even more demanding. Fifty years ago, our Catholic faith and Christian values were more respected by society in general. In addition, social media and the Internet had not dawned, and cell phones were not available to children.

Unlike 50 years ago, today's society ignores and disregards our Catholic tradition, and many of the values our children are exposed to on TV, in school, on the Internet, and through social media are in conflict with our Catholic principles. Some authors write that we live in a post-Christian world where Judeo-Christian values no longer define the culture. Other forces, like the currents in a river, are influencing our lives and shaping what we believe. As a society, we are drifting away from God. Sad to say, this is a phenomenon that is experienced in all developed countries today.

Pope Francis, speaking to the Roman Curia in 2019, said, "Christendom no longer exists! Today we are no longer the only ones who create culture, nor are we in the forefront or those most listened to… faith is often rejected, derided, marginalized and ridiculed" (12-21-1919). Catholic children attending public schools or visiting friends are exposed to situations that do not align with what they are taught at home. These experiences can confuse them. Parents need to be able to guide young inquisitive minds in the right direction.

The challenge faced by today's families is well expressed in a metaphor used by Dr. William Doherty. He writes in his book, *The Intentional Family*, that starting a family is like launching a canoe into a great river, one that is fraught by many colliding currents. If you enter the waters without a clear plan and direction for your journey, the currents will take over your life, and you will not know where you will end up. To make progress in navigating the river of life, parents need to have a destination, a plan for how to get there, and the strength to paddle hard to stay on course. Raising a family is an intentional journey.

I hope this book can help you decide what your destination is, develop a plan to get there, and find the strength to paddle hard. Maggie, the grandmother I met 50 years ago, had a plan for her grandchildren, and she was trying hard to stay on course. Maggie was intentional about raising her family Catholic. Today, to raise a Catholic family, you too must be intentional. I want to repeat this because it is important: Raising a family to be Catholic today must be intentional. It requires a conscious decision to develop habits of prayer, regular attendance to the sacraments, and loving interaction among the members of our family that help build a home environment – a family culture in which faith is practiced and is passed on by example. Just going about life without making a conscious effort to pass on the faith, or just doing what everyone else does, can weaken our faith and cause the next generation to grow distant from the religious practices that give direction and meaning to our life as Catholics in a culture that is increasingly less Christian.

The loss of faith is detrimental to your children's mental, physical and spiritual wellbeing. An article published by the Marriage and Religion Research Institute (2-13-2021) reports the findings from studies in the fields of psychology, psychiatry, and medicine on the influence of religion in our life. The researchers state that persons who practice their religion show greater ability to cope with the stresses and the hardships they encounter in their lives and are less likely to report depression, anxiety, suicide, and substance abuse.

Pope Francis told parents on the occasion of the baptism of their children: "The important thing is to transmit the faith with your life of faith; that they see the love between the spouses, that they see peace at home, that they see that Jesus is there." (1-13-2019)

Make Room for Jesus in Your Home

Making a plan for your family's journey to holiness starts with inviting God, the Father, the Son, and the Holy Spirit to be the navigator of your family's canoe. Invite Jesus to make the voyage with you and make room for him in your home.

When I was in the fifth grade and living in northern Italy, one morning after serving Mass, my pastor asked me, "Will you ask your parents if you can go with me to bless homes today?" So early that afternoon, we set out. I still see us walking on a small dusty country road. The priest wore his black cassock with a surplice, a white knee-length vestment. He had a black three-pointed hat called the biretta on his head, and he held a book in his hand. I walked alongside carrying a container with holy water. He said, "Today, we will visit the farmhouses just outside of town." At each stop, the priest gathered the families living there, whoever was not in the fields, and explained that he had come to bless their homes. This was an annual event, and they were expecting him.

The people, mostly women and children and older persons living at the farm, assembled in the largest room, and the pastor explained, "Remember that we bless your houses each year to rededicate your homes and your families to God. God lives here with you. Let's make room for him."

The pastor's message to his flock, "God lives here with you. Let's make room for him," has remained with me to this day. I hear it echoed in the words of Pope Francis, "The Lord's presence dwells in real and concrete families, with all their daily troubles and struggles, joys and hopes" (AL 315).

These words, I believe, apply to all of our families. God dwells with us and fills our lives and our homes with truly amazing graces. It does not make a difference if our rooms are messy or clean, big or small; if our family relationships are peaceful or strained. Regardless of where we are in life, God is with us. The messiness of our lives and of our homes is our problem. God stands by us with his graces, waiting for us to turn to him for help. "Remember that you are never alone. Christ is with you on your journey every day of your lives" (St. John Paul II, 8-23-1997).

The two stories just recalled, the one of Maggie, and that of my pastor, capture the message of this book. Like Maggie, we as parents need to be intentional about passing our faith to our children. And, like my pastor said to his parishioners, we need to make room for God in our lives and in our homes.

The Plan

I wrote this book to help you develop a plan for your family's journey. It contains reflections and suggestions for action on six aspects of a Catholic family's home life. The book will help you:

1. **Make your home a sanctuary** – a place where your children feel safe and welcomed.

2. **Make your home a place where Love resides**—where the goodness of God's love touches your children through your love for them. The place where God first reveals himself to your children, and they learn to relate to him.

3. **Make your home a school of prayer**—where your children learn to converse with God through simple prayer rituals, and through their gradual participation in the sacramental life of their Catholic community.

4. **Make your home an apprenticeship to loving**—a place where your children learn to love by watching how you love. Following your example, they form habits that will influence their relationships for the rest of their life.

5. **Make your home a place where children learn to live in God's time**—the place where they learn about God's providence, and that time is a precious gift to be used to serve God. Make your home a place where your family celebrates its milestones (i.e.: birthdays, anniversaries and special events) and the liturgical seasons with a sense of gratitude toward God.

6. **Make your home a training camp for discipleship**—a way of life that teaches your children that they belong to a larger family, and that true love and faith are gifts that we are to share beyond the walls of our house.

The purpose of this book is to help parents, regardless of their circumstances, create a home environment that acknowledges God's presence and helps the children learn habits that will help them grow as human beings and mature in faith.

Family spirituality is about learning to live in God's presence, letting him guide us, and giving glory to him through everything we do. This is every family's path to holiness. St. Paul writes, "Whatever you do, do from the heart, as for the Lord and not for others" (Col. 3:23).

A Word of Hope

If you are among those whose experience of home-life during your formative years has left you with painful memories, perhaps this book can help you heal.

Who Is the Book For?

This book is for all families, especially those with young children. It is for multigenerational families; families with two parents; families headed by a single mother or a single father; families where one parent is not Catholic, and for grandparents, especially those who are helping raise their grandchildren. God is in all of our homes. The Church is a family of families (AL 87). All families belong to it, and each family is unique and different.

Our homes are truly the cradle of the Church. The well-being of our home life today is critical to the future of the Church and of society. St. John Paul II said repeatedly, and his words have been echoed by Benedict XVI and Pope Francis, "The future of the world and of the church passes through the family" (FC 75).

What children learn in their homes during their formative years gives shape to their spiritual DNA and will remain with them for the rest of their lives. The researchers at the Institute for Family Studies reported in December 2021 in a paper titled "The Religious Marriage Paradox" that children who grow up in a home where faith is practiced have greater odds of a stable marriage and lower chances of divorce.

The chapters that follow are written in simple language with no big words or complicated ideas. Only simple truths that hopefully will resonate with you and practical suggestions to help your family members remember that God, the Father, Son, and Holy Spirit, is right by you all the time.

According to Church statistics (CARA 2015), approximately one-fourth of Catholic families (24%) today have a parent who is not Catholic. Recent data suggest that this number is increasing. When parents are practicing two different faiths, this disparity can, at times, create difficulties in passing on the Catholic faith. This book does not address those difficulties but points to ways in which the children can benefit from their parents' religious faiths. While it is important that children be formed in the Catholic tradition, it may be beneficial for them to be exposed to the religious and spiritual practices of the non-Catholic parent. Because this book is intended to unite and not divide families, you will find across all the chapters reflection questions and conversation starters that, in most cases, can be answered by both parents.

How to Use This Book

Mother and father can ideally use the book together. However, if your spouse is not interested or not able to read the book, do not be discouraged. Do it alone. You are a co-parent, and you can contribute to creating a home environment for your family that fosters growth in faith. In other words, you are co-responsible for setting the direction for your children's Christian formation. This book can also be used by groups of parents, such as those organized by a Catholic school or by a parish during the preparation for the sacraments: Baptism, First Confession, or First Communion; or by groups of parents who meet regularly. It can also be used by small groups sponsored by Lay Ecclesial Movements such as the Christian Family Movement, Teams of Our Lady, Couples for Christ, Marriage Encounter, the Cursillo Movement, Christ Renews His Parish, and other such ministries.

The pages that follow are intended to be savored, reflected upon, and discussed. Read one chapter at a time, and reflect on the questions you find throughout it. Many of these are intended for your own development. Each chapter closes with a call to action. This is your opportunity to identify small actions your family can take to improve your home environment and set the direction for your children's spiritual growth. In addition, each chapter ends with a set of "conversation starters" and suggestions to help you engage your children in thoughtful conversations that will help them grow in the

Catholic faith.

What This Book Is Not

The chapters of this book reflect the spirituality of the Christian family developed in our Catholic tradition over the centuries. Therefore, what is proposed here is not a throwback to an earlier way of life that is not fitting for modern times. The content of this book is inspired by the words of St. John Paul II, "Catholic Parents must learn to form their family as a 'domestic church,' a church in the home as it were, where God is honored, his law is respected, prayer is a normal event, virtue is transmitted by word and example, and everyone shares the hopes, the problems, and sufferings of everyone else. All this is not to advocate a return to some outdated style of living: it is to return to the roots of human development and human happiness" (Homily at Aqueduct Racetrack in Brooklyn, NY, 10- 6-1995).

This book is not a set of prescriptions for Catholic families to adopt. In other words, what you will read is not prescriptive; it is descriptive. It describes the author's and other people's experiences of growing up in a Catholic home. Your experiences may be different from theirs. I encourage you to take from these pages what is useful to you and your family. Consider what the book is suggesting and adapt it to your own situation. I hope these pages will help you carry out the responsibilities you accepted on the day you asked the Church to baptize your children, and you promised to pass on our Catholic faith to them.

To assist you, the book contains an Appendix with a short list of traditional Catholic prayers.

Suggestion:

At the end of each chapter, you will find a call to action and suggestions for what you can do. I want to invite you to embrace the first call to action: a simple blessing of your home. This is a worthy prayer. Recall the words of my pastor, "We bless your houses each year to rededicate your homes and your families to God."

Years ago, there were more priests, and it was possible for them to visit families to bless their parishioners' homes. Today, in the United States, it is still possible to ask your pastor or deacon to come to bless your home, but their time availability is limited. If you live in a community where it is easy to schedule a home blessing with a priest or deacon, I encourage you to do so. If this is not easily done, I would encourage you to use the short home blessing on the next page. Do it with your family and explain, as my pastor did to his parishioners, that we do this ritual to dedicate our home and our family to God. We do it to remember that we are part of his family, and he lives among us. He is the guide on our family's journey.

This home blessing is adapted from the custom known as "Chalking of the Door." Through this simple ritual, we ask God's blessing on those who live in the home and on all those who visit throughout the year. Make this an annual ritual for your family that you can repeat each New Year's Day, or on the day of the Epiphany.

Home Blessing

Gather by your home's entrance, the front door of your apartment or house. Then the head of the family or any member leads.

Let us pray!

In the name of the Father, the Son, and the Holy Spirit. Amen.

Lord our God,

come and bless this house (apartment) which is our home.

Surround this shelter with Your Holy Spirit.

Encompass all its four sides with the power of Your protection

so that no evil or harm will come near.

May the divine blessing shield this home from destruction, storm, sickness and all that might bring evil to us who shall live within these walls.

Then, using some chalk, preferably blessed, (you can take the chalk to Mass and have it blessed by a priest or deacon) write the following on the entrance to your home: +20 CMB 23+. The numbers represent the year, in the example 2023. The letters CMB stand for "Christus Mansionem Benedicat," a Latin phrase that means "May Christ bless this dwelling." Some carry out this blessing on the occasion of the Epiphany and interpret the letters CMB to represent the names of the three kings: **C**aspar, **M**elchior and **B**althasar. After writing these numbers and letters, continue your prayer.

Blessed be this doorway.

May all who come to it be treated with respect and kindness.

May all our comings and goings be under the seal of God's loving care.

Blessed be all the rooms of this home.

May each of them be holy and filled with the spirit of happiness.

May no dark powers ever be given shelter within any of these rooms but banished as soon as recognized.

Let us pray as our Lord taught us to pray: (Recite together the Our Father...)

May God's holy blessing rest upon us all,

In the name of the Father, and the Son, and of the Holy Spirit. Amen.

The prayer is adapted from Prayers for the Domestic Church by Edward Hays. Copyright 2007 by Ave Maria Press, P.O. Box 428, Notre Dame, IN 46556. Used with permission of publisher.

Track Your Family's Journey

Your family is on a journey. Use this book to guide your household on the chosen path, and track your progress by documenting the actions you decide to take after reading each chapter.

1.   Home Is Our Sanctuary

ACTION:

2.   Home Is Where Love Resides

ACTION:

3. Home Is a School of Prayer

ACTION:

4. Home Is an Apprenticeship to Loving

ACTION:

5. Home Is Where We Learn to Live in God's Time

ACTION:

6. Home Is a Training Camp for Discipleship

ACTION:

CHAPTER 1

HOME IS OUR SANCTUARY

Home

Home is a word that has a special meaning for everyone. Many poems have been written about "home." If I could summarize the sentiments of the poets, it would be that home is a refuge and the place where love resides. It is where we find peace. Here is one example.

> *Better than gold is a peaceful home,*
> *Where all the fire side characters come,*
> *The shrine of love, the heavens of life…*

"Better than Gold"-- Fr. Abram Joseph Ryan

We all want our home to be what poets sing: a shrine of love, a heaven of life. The reality is that home is, for all of us, a work in progress. We all know what we wish our home to be, but making it happen requires work and sacrifice because home is founded on love, and learning to love demands self-mastery and self-giving, and that is a journey of a lifetime.

Fr. Ryan, quoted above, states that home is "The shrine of love." Home is a "shrine," a sanctuary." The terms "shrine" and "sanctuary" can be understood as a place of refuge and protection and also as a sacred space - a place of prayer. In this chapter we will address our home as a refuge, a place of safety, especially for our children, in the next we will consider our home as a sacred space.

Our Home Is Our Haven

Home is the place we go to for protection and healing; "the heavens of life," as described by the poet, Fr. Ryan. After a long day at work, we return home to connect with the love of our family members and to recharge. For many of us, home is the place we long to return after having been away. Who has not experienced the comfort of returning home after a long trip, a hard day at work, or being away to contend with a crisis of some sort?

I fondly remember the years when I traveled monthly for business to places around the world: Europe, Central, and South America, Asia, and Australia. I loved to travel and to meet people from different cultures, and to work side by side with them. But what I loved even more was coming back home to rest and, most of all, to feel the love of my family. For me, arriving home began when my plane touched down at the airport in my hometown. I felt joy, and I looked forward to being welcomed by my wife Teri, who was waiting for me in the terminal. Home is the place that helps me remember who I am. Home is my refuge, my sanctuary, and my point of reference in my life.

Where do you call home right now?

A few years ago, Teri and I took our daughters and grandson with us to Italy to visit our Italian family. Our grandson was eight at the time, and to prepare him for the trip, we talked to him about the places and people he would visit: The Alps, Venice, family members, his cousins, and many other planned experiences. One day, Teri asked him, "After we land in Italy, what will you look forward to doing?" He promptly answered, "Coming home!" He did go with us and had a great time meeting and playing with his Italian cousins, but home remained his secure point of reference. In fact, each evening, to stay connected with home, he would call his dad, who had remained there because he could not travel.

Home is also a place we turn to when we need protection. I remember when our daughters were very young and played in the neighborhood with their friends, if they got hurt or felt wronged, they would run home crying, seeking comfort and justice; someone to take their side and understand how they felt.

Some days, even at my age, I feel the same way. I come home seeking someone to just listen to me and understand what I have been through and how I feel. Do you feel the same way?

Reflection:

- On what occasions do you feel that your home is your refuge?
- Do you remember situations when, as a child, you went home seeking protection, understanding, or justice?

Home Is Where Children Need To Feel Safe

To feel secure, children need to sense that their parents can provide a safe physical and emotional space. Children need to know that their parents can take care of their needs and are united in their efforts. Pope Francis writes to parents, "Children need a sense of security that can enable them to have confidence in you, and in the certainty that they will never be alone, whatever may come their way" (Letter to Couples, 12-26-2021). Did you feel safe in your childhood home?

One of the things that scares children is conflict between their parents. I have seen the confusion on our young daughters' faces when Teri and I had a disagreement and they happened to be present. Conflicts in a marriage are inevitable; in fact, I would venture to say that they are necessary for the growth of the couple. The mingling of two personalities with different family histories is not an easy task. It requires years of negotiating with a lot of patience and determination.

Marriage is a wonderful vocation. Your relationship is like gold that needs to be refined, and happiness together comes from a lifetime of refining. It is inescapable that your children will be exposed to your conflicts, but if they witness the conflicts, they also need to see that love remains and all is right.

With the permission of the author Erica Chambers, I want to share a verse from a song written by her that describes the feelings of a child. As a young child, the artist suffered much because of her parents' disagreements. The title of the song is "All is Right." Here are her words:

> *Last night I saw you kiss her on the porch*
> *I watched you from the window*
> *Just before I turned my covers down.*
> *Now I can go to sleep and know that everything is right*
> *With the world, with the night*
> *All is right.*

Managing Conflicts

Although disagreements are perfectly normal, sometimes it is easy to get stuck in ways of handling conflicts that are destructive and hurt the family. In his book *Why Marriages Succeed or Fail*, Dr. Gottman, a noted researcher, identifies four behaviors that should be red flags to every couple.

- **Criticism**: when you blame your spouse and attack their personality or character. It often starts with "You always…" or "You never…"

- **Contempt**: when you find yourself calling your spouse names with the intent of hurting and humiliating. It projects and attitude of superiority.

- **Defensiveness**: when feeling attacked, you react by making excuses or attacking back.

- **Stonewalling**: when one of you shuts down and walks away, leaving the conflict unresolved and tension in the air.

Dr. Gottman calls these behaviors the Four Horsemen of the Apocalypse because when they are present in a marriage and become habits, they take over the relationship and bring about its demise.

Through his extensive research on marriage relationships, Dr. Gottman writes in his book: *The Seven Principles for Making Marriage Work* that in a marriage 69% of conflicts are not solvable and are recurring. Successful couples deal with them by learning to tolerate each other's quirks, and by accepting each person's uniqueness with a good attitude. Among the recurring conflicts are those arising from differences in personal preferences: one person likes the room warm, the other cold; or one person has a preference for socializing, the other for quiet time; or one has a preference for planning things, the other for spontaneity.

On the other hand, there are conflicts that can be resolved, and this can be done without causing damage to the relationship. Dr. Gottman suggests five skills:

1. **Soften Your Startup.** To ensure that you will be heard by your spouse, take personal responsibility for what you feel or what you wish, then start the conversation with "I" instead of "You." Don't blame your spouse. Just describe what you feel or think. For example: "I feel frustrated when I look for something and I cannot find it. Have you used the scissors lately? That is better than attacking your spouse with: "Where did you put the scissors?" Or an accusation, "You never put things back where they belong!"

2. **Learn to Make and Receive Repair Attempts.** When the conversation starts off on a wrong foot and you find yourself

becoming defensive, it is important to find a way to de-escalate the tension. To repair the damage, change the tone of the conversation with words such as: "I am sorry, I did not intend to insult you or make you feel uncomfortable." Or, "I am feeling very defensive right now with the way this conversation is going. Can we take a break?"

3. **If Necessary, Take a Break to Calm Yourselves Down.** Gottman suggests that when spouses become too emotional to be objective, it is better for them to take a short break to calm themselves down. Give yourselves at least twenty minutes to recompose yourselves so that you can return to the conversation with a frame of mind that allows you to listen and to understand each other's points of view.

4. **Seek a Compromise.** Dr. Gottman writes that conflict resolution is not about one person changing, or trying to change the other. It's about seeking a common ground, negotiating and finding a way to accommodate each other. No none gets all they want, but both feel respected and understood.

5. **Be Tolerant of Each Other's Faults.** Gottman writes: "Until you accept your partner's flaws and foibles, you will not be able to compromise successfully. Instead, you will be on a relentless campaign to alter your spouse."

The process of learning to live with or to resolve the conflicts we encounter in our family is one that is facilitated by effective communication. A most important task in communicating is that of listening. The listening needed is not just hearing what our spouse is saying, but seeking to understand what our spouse or children are telling us. This listening is difficult because in the process of listening we encounter many obstacles from within us, such as: our emotions at the moment, our impulse to interrupt our spouse or children to tell them what we want or how we feel, or preparing our rebuttal in our mind while the other person is talking. Time can also be a factor. If we are in a hurry, and our mind is on what is coming next, it is difficult to be in the present and to listen. In learning to listen and to deal with our conflicts our faith can be helpful. Ask the Holy Spirit to give you the patience you need to put your spouse first and truly listen. Then, let go of your defensiveness and seek to understand.

Terrence and Michele are a married couple that shared some of their growing pains with a group of engaged couples during a retreat. They told their audience that they had both been married before and shortly after their wedding they found themselves growing distant due to frequent arguments and disagreements. "It felt like we were always mad," said Michele. Each one of them had brought many habits, preferences and assumptions from their previous married and single life, and these were clashing, causing a lot of pain.

Fortunately, Terrence and Michele had the wisdom to stop themselves before they caused more damage to the relationship and decided to seek some mutual understanding. The first step was to identify what each did that cause pain to the other. They devised a calendar with three columns: a column for the plusses, (things you did today that pleased me) and one for the minuses, (things that you did today that grated on me.) Another column was for interactions that were neutral. At the end of each day, they shared their thoughts.

For example, one day, Michele wrote in the positive column a: *"[Terrence] called about the license plate. Cleaned up living room – thanks! Really nice evening! Heart you."* In the negative column she wrote: *"Wanders to another project – leaving another project not cleaned up – drives me crazy – especially when there is a lot I want to get done in little time – felt like your 'mother'."* Terrence replied, *"Give me a chance – a lot of those projects are related to each other anyway, Mom!"* Then he wrote about what Michele did that made him happy: *"[She] worked very hard on house/dinner. Went to store, prepared for Sunday visit, nice night out with Matthew…"*

The couple found that documenting the sources of their hurts and their joys and sharing them allowed them to get to know each other better. This growth in mutual understanding and appreciation made it easier for them to accommodate one another and to compromise. This approach gradually helped them eliminate some of the more significant sources of pain and affirmed the positive in the relationship. Prayer guided them and sustained them and with the help of the Holy Spirit they learned to love.

There Is Help

If you find that when differences with your spouse arise you are unable to resolve a conflict that is causing damage to the relationship, it may be time to take notice of your difficulty and bring this problem to your spouse's attention, and if necessary, seek professional help.

Teri and I turned for help to counselors when we faced difficult moments in our 50 years of marriage. One such moment was when I was downsized, and we did not know what was ahead for our family. We were both anxious, stressed out, and often short with each other and with the children. We needed to come to an agreement on a common path forward for our family. Unfortunately, each one of us felt stuck in our personal grief and could not recognize the other's needs. Eventually, we accepted that we could not get out of this rut by ourselves, so we reached out to professionals for guidance. With the help of God's grace and the counsel of trained personnel, we sailed through the storm.

Sometimes a few sessions with a counselor, who can mediate your differences and help you identify what is causing your pain, can be enough to put your relationship back on track. Do it for your children! They deserve a home that provides for them a safe place. The quality of your marriage relationship sets the tone for life in your home. Your relationship is the foundation of the domestic church that resides at your address.

If you are a single parent, you, too, can provide the refuge in your home that your children crave. Be attentive to their needs and guard against expressing your anger for your "ex" in front of the children or to them. Your children need to know that they are safe with either parent.

When the physical and emotional environment of the home is full of tension and uncertainty, it becomes more difficult to address the spiritual needs of the children. A home environment that is safe and welcoming is the first step in building a Catholic home life.

Reflection:

- How do your children react when they are exposed to a conflict between you and your spouse?
- What works and what does not work for you in the way you resolve your differences with your spouse?
- If you are a single parent, what is causing your children anxiety today?

Another Aspect of Safety – Setting Boundaries

Another way that parents help their children feel safe and secure in their home is by setting healthy boundaries. Boundaries protect the child and teach them that the world does not revolve around them and they cannot always have what they want.

Krissy Pozatek, MSW, an author and therapist, writes that unfortunately today in many homes children's voices and opinions equal those of their parents. While it is important to listen to children' opinions and emotions, for a home environment to be stable and secure parents still need to be in charge. Parents are responsible for setting boundaries and expectations. When boundaries are not clear or not enforced it gives rise to feelings of anxiety, according to Pozatek. Children feel anxious when they perceive that parents are not in charge.

A blog on All Pro Dad website lists ways to establish clear

boundaries for children. I am listing five:

1. Be trustworthy – Kids need to know that you mean what you say. Keep your word.
2. Keep the rules simple.
3. Involve the child in boundary setting.
4. Be precise – ensure the rules are clear and the child understands them.
5. Recognize appropriate behavior – reinforce the good behavior.

One area where boundaries are important in protecting the child's spiritual wellbeing is that of managing the use of media. I want to share Pope Francis' word of advice to parents on this regard.

"Parents need to consider what they want their children to be exposed to, and this necessarily means being concerned about who is providing their entertainment, who is entering their rooms through television and electronic devices, and with whom they are spending their free time. Only if we devote time to our children, speaking of important things with simplicity and concern, and finding healthy ways for them to spend their time, will we be able to shield them from harm. Vigilance is always necessary and neglect is never beneficial" (AL 260).

Reflection:

- How do you manage your children's use of TV, cell phones, Internet, social media, and gaming?

Action:

Whether you are a co-parent or a single parent, you know that reflection and conversation are good, but without action, little progress is made in a family. As you conclude this chapter, you are encouraged to make a simple resolution. Agree with your family members on one small action that you will take as a result of having read this chapter. When choosing your action, consider the suggestions below, and encourage other ideas from members of your family. Keep it easy and simple!

Write your plan here:

_____

I encourage you to track your family's journey as suggested on page 12 of the Introduction.

Suggestions:

1. With the help of your spouse, identify situations in your home and in your marriage relationship that may cause anxiety to your children.
2. Agree with your spouse how you want to handle your disagreements, especially when the children are present.
3. Consider ways you could both improve your listening to each other and grow in mutual understanding.
4. Ask your children what causes them to feel anxious at home, at school, or in other places.
5. Review your family's rules about the use of cell phone, TV, Internet, social media, gaming and song lyrics.
6. Review your family's rules about friends, and sleep-overs.

Conversation Starters for Families

Below are topics for conversation with your children on the subject of feeling secure at home. You, as a parent or a grandparent, can bring these subjects up during informal chats at home, during car rides, or during meals. Use the questions below as conversation starters. Word them in a way that is appropriate for each child's age.

1. "What do you like the most about our life at home?"
2. "When are you happiest?"
3. "When are you most sad?"
4. "What scares you or makes you feel uncomfortable at home or at school and other places."
5. "If you could change anything at home, what would it be?"
6. "What friends or schoolmates make you feel uncomfortable? What do they say or do?"
7. "When your friends disagree with you, how do you feel? Are you still a friend with them?"
8. "How do you feel when we (mom and dad) disagree?"
9. In our home we have certain rules about the use of TV, cell phones, Internet and social media. "Do you remember what they are? Why do you think we have these rules?"

Conversation Starters for Parents or Groups

<u>Notes for the group leader:</u>
-Begin the meeting with the prayer to the Holy Family (end of Chapter 1).
-Start the conversation with a general question, such as: what did you find interesting and helpful in this chapter? What story touched you the most? What anecdotes or situations from your own life came to mind as you read the chapter?
-Continue the conversation by using the questions below.
-Close the meeting by asking participants to identify one thing they want to remember from the chapter or from the conversation that just took place.

1. How safe do you think your family feels in your home?
2. In your opinion, what contributes to providing a safe and secure home environment for your children?
3. What causes anxiety to your children?
4. How would you know if your children have been exposed to bullying or intimidation?
5. How do your children react when they are exposed to a conflict between their parents?
6. What works well for you in resolving conflicts between you and your spouse, such as: when differences in preferences, opinions, habits and personal quirks seem to clash?
7. How do you manage the use of TV, cell phones, the Internet, social media and gaming in your home?
8. How would you guard against the influence on your children from others whose points of view and values you disapprove?
9. What boundaries do you create to protect your children?

Prayer

The home of the Holy Family was a sacred and holy space because Jesus, the Son of God, was physically present. Mary and Joseph are model spouses and parents: obedient to God's will, faithful, generous, responsible, and chaste. I invite you to say the **Prayer to the Holy Family** found on the Appendix, or **A Parent's Prayer**, found below.

A Parent's Prayer

Loving God,

You are the giver of all we possess,
the source of all of our blessings.
We thank and praise you.

Thank you for the gift of our children.

Help us to set boundaries for them,
and yet encourage them to explore.
Give us the strength and courage to treat
each day as a fresh start.

May our children come to know you, the one true God,
and Jesus Christ, whom you have sent.

May your Holy Spirit help them to grow
in faith, hope, and love,
so they may know peace, truth, and goodness.

May their ears hear your voice.
May their eyes see your presence in all things.
May their lips proclaim your word.
May their hearts be your dwelling place.
May their hands do works of charity.
May their feet walk in the way of Jesus Christ,
your Son and our Lord.
Amen.

CHAPTER 2

HOME IS WHERE LOVE RESIDES

Sacred Spaces

In the poem quoted in Chapter 1, Fr. Ryan calls home "The shrine of love." Home is a shrine - a sanctuary. A family's home is a sanctuary, a sacred space – a place where we meet God.

Across history, humanity has set aside spaces that have a spiritual significance and meaning, and we call these "sacred." Today, each community has sacred spaces that remind those who live there that there is a world beyond us. People go to these consecrated places to seek a connection with the transcendent; to remind themselves that they do not have all the answers—they are not God. They go to worship, to listen, to express appreciation, to find guidance and the courage to carry on.

As I mentioned earlier, in my career, I spent over twenty years traveling internationally for my employers to many countries across the globe. I would go there to meet and work with the local employees. In my spare time, I would visit the tourist sites and the sacred buildings in their communities. In Western Europe, I saw many beautiful churches and shrines with steeples whose bells marked the hours of the day and called the believers to prayer. In Russia, I was struck by the beauty of the onion-shaped domes of the Orthodox churches and the colorful icons decorating their interior. In Japan, I visited Shinto shrines with their rituals and large bells and drums whose deep sounds spread a sense of awe and mystery in the air. In Thailand, the city of Bangkok is dotted with the golden roofs of Buddhist temples, in which visitors are invited to remove their shoes and proceed with quiet reverence. In Indonesia and the Middle East, I was awakened by the sound of the muezzin's call to prayer. In India, I paused barefoot in silent reflection at Hindu temples.

Perhaps you, too, have traveled and visited sacred spaces in the United States or abroad. In your own community, you can find sacred buildings and spaces, such as the church at your parish or mission, local shrines and chapels dedicated to Mary or the saints, the cathedral in your diocese, and the hallowed grounds of your local cemetery.

Your home is a sacred space – a place where we meet God.

Reflection:

- What sacred spaces (churches or shrines) have you found most inspiring?

Your Home Is a Sacred Space

Pope Francis wrote in Amoris Laetitia: "The Lord's presence dwells in real and concrete families, with all their daily troubles and struggles, joys and hopes" (AL 315) God is present in your family. His presence makes your home a sacred space. In an effort to remind ourselves of this reality, we often decorate our homes with sacred images and religious artifacts.

A few years ago, my wife and I purchased a lot for our retirement home. The new house was being built not far from where we lived, so we visited the location daily to check on the progress. One day, while there, we met the builder who gave us a tour and an update on the project. Before leaving, he said, "Tomorrow, we will start putting up the sheetrock to create the walls." Teri asked, "Could I write a Scripture passage on the studs over the sink in the kitchen?" "Yes, of course," said the builder. Then he continued, "I know a family that wrote Bible passages all over their house before the walls went up."

Inspired by his words, we went home, and Teri pulled out the family Bible, and we started writing our favorite passages on a piece of paper. Then we returned to the site to leave our permanent mark on the structure. By the front door, Teri wrote, "As you enter a house wish it peace" (Matt. 10:12). Next to it, she wrote the words of the Jewish Shema, "Hear, o Israel: The Lord our God, the Lord is One" (Deut. 6:4). In our bedroom, she wrote, "Nights and days bless the Lord, praise and exalt him above all forever" (Dan. 3:71). In the kitchen, facing the view overlooking the woods and the fields, she wrote, "Lord, it is good that we are here" (Matt. 17:4). This last passage had been a source of consolation to her during difficult times, especially when I lost my job and we had to relocate twice.

For us, marking our home with Bible passages was a form of blessing of our dwelling. Once the house was built and we had moved in, we invited a deacon from our parish to come and bless our home.

Catholic families remind themselves of God's presence among them in the way they decorate their homes. When entering a Catholic dwelling one notices crucifixes, images or icons, statues of Mary and the saints, holy water fonts, candles and shrines. These images are reminders, they are not idols; they are expressions of a family's faith. The crucifix, for example, represents Christ's sacrificial love that saved us. The images and statues of Mary and the saints prompt us to remember that through our baptism we have become, in Christ, members of a large spiritual family, a family of holy people who are ready to intercede for us. These are our spiritual friends. As we decorate our home with photos of our earthly friends and family members, we also decorate with images of our spiritual family. We will refer to these blessed religious artifacts as sacramentals, in Chapter 3.

Our homes are sacred spaces. They are sacred not because we decorate them with religious images. Decorations do not make our home more holy. There is nothing we can do to make our home holy. Our home is a sacred space because God lives there with our family, as Pope Francis reminds us, "God dwells in us, with us, and among us" (Letter to Couples: 12-26-2021). Our home is truly the place where God, who is Love resides, and we bathe in his love daily. Religious images and decorations help us create a home environment that reminds us that God is present.

Reflection:

- If I walked into your home today, what Catholic images and decorations would I see? What do they mean to you?
- What are your earliest memories of your home life as a child? What were your best experiences of life and love in your childhood home?

My Experience of Home

When I was a young boy in Italy, my family surrounded me with an environment filled with love and faith. It was a gift from Divine Providence. For that, I am grateful. I grew up in a home where the Catholic way of life was all that I knew. My home was decorated with pictures of family members and with images of members of our spiritual family: Jesus, Mary, and the saints. My family said prayers before going to bed and before meals and the rosary from time to time. We attended Mass every Sunday and sometimes during the week. Illness was the only excuse for missing Sunday Mass. Our parents monitored our behavior and language and corrected us when disrespectful. I expect that many of my readers were raised in a similar home environment to one degree or another.

Having grown up in Italy in the 1950s, I was fortunate that my whole town was my extended Catholic family. The small city of 20,000 had four parishes and eight priests. Today, streets are still named after saints, and along the roads, one can still find small shrines to Mary or to a patron saint. The church bells awakened us in the morning. They called us to Mass, and during the day, they invited us to pray the Angelus in the morning, noon, and evening. When someone died, the bells sent out a somber sound that reminded the town to pray for the soul of the departed.

I do not want to give the impression that my home was perfect. Far from it. We had our storms. I fought regularly with my brother and my sister. My parents and grandparents lived in the same household and experienced the stresses of living as an extended family in very small quarters. Although we were a faith-filled family, each member had their own unique personality and imperfections that created conflicts and misunderstandings. My grandmother was always very outspoken and full of advice for her daughter, my mother. This was grating on both of my parents, but especially on my father, who did not want his mother-in-law to dictate how he should raise his family. He resented it but would not challenge her in front of us children. These were human beings with very different personalities trying to make the best of their situation in spite of their imperfections.

As children, we felt deeply loved both by our parents and grandparents, and their faith and example showed us what it means to be a good person. The words "I am sorry" and "forgive me" were spoken often, and so was "Thank you!"

What was helpful to all of us as a family during the good times and the bad days was our Catholic faith. Through it, we welcomed God into our home, and through prayer and reflection, we let him guide our actions. The faith of my family continues to sustain me today. I remember that in the early years of our marriage, my grandmother and my father used to write to Teri and me in the United States. They would give us news about our family and our friends and would always close with a piece of advice and a request, "Be good, and please pray for us. We are praying for you!"

Years later, I asked my father what advice he would like to pass on to his granddaughters. He wrote, "What is important in life is to be humble, to help those who are in need, and to love everyone. To be successful in life be always honest, act as a gentleman, whether you are an hourly worker, or a salesclerk or an executive. Follow your conscience and pray. The prayers I found most helpful in my life are the Our Father and the Rosary, which I pray every day." That was the legacy that my father, a man with a fifth-grade education, wanted me to pass on to his grandchildren.

Reflection:

- What role did faith play in your family as you were growing up?
- If your experience of home life has not been positive, consider how you can heal and make peace with your past. Focus your attention on what you want your home life to be from now on. What is your dream and your hope?

Home is Where We Are Touched by Love

When we read the Pope's words: "The Lord's presence dwells in real and concrete families," (AL 315) we may ask ourselves: how do I know it? How do we know that God is in our home? God is invisible, and we cannot perceive his presence with our senses. As Catholics we believe that God dwells in a special way within the hearts of the baptized. In addition, the Scriptures and our Catholic tradition tell us that God is love and he is present where love is. St. John the Evangelist tells us, "Beloved, let us love one another, because love is of God." 1 Jn 4:7. According to the poet Fr. Ryan, our home is the "shrine of love." God is Love. He lives in our homes, and we can taste, although imperfectly, the goodness of his love in the love of our family members. Through your love God touches your children in a real way to express his love for them. That is how they will know what it means to be loved by God.

Think about your childhood—do you remember moments when you felt total joy in the company of your parents or grandparents? I remember the good feelings I had when, as a young child, I held my mother's hand while walking on the streets of my hometown. I felt secure because I was connected to her. I felt important when I sat on my grandmother's lap and was held by her. I was filled with joy because I was the center of her attention. And, as I grew up, I felt affirmed when my father would ask me to help him with a project because he thought I was big enough to handle the task. I also remember vividly the day, when as a teenager, growing up in Italy, I was sitting with my father at a train station, and he asked me, "Do you want a beer?" I was surprised by his offer. "I think you are old enough," he said. He ordered a beer for himself and shared a small glass with me. This was my first. I did not like the taste of the beer, but I drank some of it because I was honored that my father thought I was old enough to share a beer with me. Have you had similar experiences? To me, these are memories of love—a love that gives me a taste of the goodness of God's love. God's love is reassuring and guiding like my mother's hand. It is the source of joy, like the embrace of my grandmother. It is affirming, like my father's acknowledgments of my growth.

God lives with us, and his presence is felt in the love we nurture in our relationships around our kitchen table. His love touches us through our expressions of caring for one another: kindness, faithfulness, fairness, tolerance, forgiveness, understanding, and generosity. Christ is present in the good times and in the difficult times, and through the Holy Spirit, he gives us the wisdom and the courage to make the sacrifices needed for the good of our spouse and our children.

Unfortunately, at times, our love seems to go dormant. Pope Francis tells us not to be afraid. God is with us. regardless of how we feel. On March 27, 2020, he compared the storms of our life (at the time, he was referring to the COVID-19 pandemic) to the storm on the Sea of Galilee encountered by Jesus and his disciples (Mark 4:35-41). Jesus was on a boat with the disciples, and he was asleep. A storm came, and the disciples were scared. When they woke him up, he said to them, "Why are you afraid? Have you no faith?" Jesus is with us in our homes during the storms of our life. He invites us to trust in him and to have faith in him. "Do not be afraid!" is a phrase Jesus said repeatedly to his disciples.

Reflection:

- Take a moment to remember times in your life, as a child, adolescent, or adult when you felt loved in a special way by a family member. How would you describe those feelings?
- Recall the times when you turned to God for strength and guidance to help you act in a loving way toward a member of your family.

Your Home Is God's Workshop

God is present in your home. In fact, we could say that your home is God's workshop. It is in the intimacy of your family that the mystery of life unfolds. You are a partner with God in the advancement of his design for humanity. Pope Francis tells us that to become parents is to "choose to dream with [God],.. to join him in this saga of building a world where no one will feel alone" (AL 321).

A friend who is an experienced pediatrician and a man of deep faith asked me one day, "Do you know what causes the glow that expecting mothers have?" I answered his question with a smile, and he continued, "There is a medical reason for it, but I prefer to think that the glow that we see reveals God's presence with the mother and her child in this important work of creation."

It is in your home that God, with your help, creates human beings--eternal souls. It is with God's help that you guide your children toward maturity. It is with God's grace that you pass on the Christian faith. It is in your home that God reveals himself to your children and shows them his love through your loving words and actions. Your children have a natural openness to the transcendent. According to Maria Montessori, in the heart of every child, there is a sense of God's existence. It is there but not conscious. We need to allow it to grow like we would help a plant grow. St Paul wrote to the Romans: "The love of God has been poured out into our hearts through the Holy Spirit." (Romans 5:5)

One evening during the Christmas season, Teri was driving in our neighborhood with our young grandson, who, at the time, was four years old. The car was passing in front of homes with many decorations. The child was transfixed by the lights and was very quiet. At one point, the car came upon a house that had a large Nativity scene in the front yard. Our grandson exclaimed in excitement, "Nonna, Nonna, (Italian name for grandmother) I see God!"

Children's eyes are open to seeing signs of God's presence in their surroundings. Jesus said, "Amen, I say to you, unless you turn and become like children you will not enter the kingdom of heaven" (Matt. 18:3).

Reflection:

- Can you think of situations in which you have noticed how your children are open to sensing God's presence, as Maria Montessori states?
- What do you have in your home that reminds you and your children of God's presence? What visible signs of your faith are displayed in your home?

The Sacraments Give Us a Special Relationship with the Trinity

For Catholic parents, the seven sacraments provide a special faith connection with God: Father, Son, and Holy Spirit. God is present in our daily life because when we were baptized, we were freed from sin, and we entered a personal relationship with the Trinity. God entered our life, and we became temples of the Holy Spirit, as St. Paul tells us, "Do you know that you are the temple of God, and that the Spirit of God dwells in you?" (1 Cor. 3:16). With God present in our life, we cannot fear the challenges of life—the challenges of parenthood.

Most people can remember times in their family when they prayed for help because they were going through a difficult time. As parents, we turn to God for help when we see our children suffer. I prayed hard one Sunday morning when our baby daughter got her hand pinched in a folding chair at church and almost severed one of her fingers. We prayed desperately one late snowy winter night when one of our teenage daughters, who was driving out of town to visit a friend, did not show up at her destination at the expected time. The friend was concerned, and so were we. Fortunately, she arrived several hours late. She had decided to go to a late movie and did not tell anyone.

The relationship with God we entered at Baptism was strengthened at Confirmation with the gift of the Holy Spirit, and it is sustained today with the regular participation in the Eucharist and the sacrament of Reconciliation.

Matrimony is also another sacrament through which you invited God into your life. For us Catholics, the wedding rite is a sacrament—a ritual through which God touches our life and transforms it. When the bride and the groom recite their vows, the Holy Spirit binds them, as the United States Catholic Bishops teach us, "The Holy Spirit binds the spouses together in a bond of love and fidelity to death" (LL p. 33). That bond is strengthened by the couple's union with Christ and the Church: "Their marriage covenant becomes a participation in the unbreakable covenant between Christ the Bridegroom and his Bride, the Church" (LL p. 33). Through their marriage covenant, the couple's life becomes intertwined with the life of the Trinity as described in a document of the Second Vatican Council: "Authentic married love is caught up into divine love, and is directed and enriched by the redemptive power of Christ's and the salvific action of the Church, so that this love may lead the spouses to God" (GS 48).

Through your union with Christ and the Church your life is touched by grace. God, the Father, Son and Holy Spirit, dwell with you. Your home is a place where God, who is Love, is first revealed to your children through your love, and through your example the Gospel message is first preached to them. Your home life is part of the life of the Church, it is the church in your home, and your family is a domestic church.

Reflection:

- What do you know about your baptism? Do you know the place where you were baptized? Do you know the date? Do you know where your baptismal certificate is?
- Recall a time when you turned to God for help because you felt powerless and helpless.
- What do you remember about your wedding?

Husband and Wife, an Icon of God's Love

In the sacred space of your home, you and your spouse, are "Living icons of God's love" says Pope Francis (4-2-14). And, St. John Paul II encourages you to "Become who you are" (FC 17). In other words, husband and wife are called to be the image of Love—of divine love. Becoming an icon of God's love is a high standard for all of us. Achieving it is a work in progress for all couples. As we struggle along, we need to remember that however imperfect, our love is the primary image of God's love that our children see as they grow up. Our children learn who Love (God) is by gazing their parents' love as spouses and as mother and father. Pope Francis, in his letter to married couples and parents, writes, "Know that your children—especially the younger ones—watch you attentively; in you they seek the sign of a strong and reliable love" (Letter to Married Couples, 12-26-2021).

Here, I want to emphasize the word "imperfect." Our marriage relationship is an imperfect icon of God's love. The fact is that there is no perfect marriage. Marriages are made up of imperfect people who are on a journey to build a life together as a man and a woman. This journey includes learning to live with each other's differences, and even imperfections. These differences are what make each marriage unique. Our differences and imperfections will remain with us until our last day.

To succeed on this journey, spouses need to rise above their differences and find common ground, which becomes their constant point of reference in spite of their varied feelings, beliefs, preferences, and habits, and together sail through the adversities they encounter.

Catholic couples find that common ground in their vocation to serve God together through their marriage. Among their primary duties are to worship God with their life, to pass on the Christian faith to the next generation, and to prepare their children to become responsible adults. This is an important task for the good of society and of the Church. This is every couple's vocation. It is their mission, the point of reference for their lives.

Today, in some families, the spouses may not share a common faith or may not practice with the same commitment. If your family is one of these, do not give up. Do all you can to collaborate with your spouse to find the spiritual common ground for your family in spite of your differences. Your children need clear and consistent direction from their parents, especially when it comes to what to believe and how to behave. This direction is expressed not only through your words of advice but mostly through your action, through your example. The graces of the sacrament of matrimony will help you.

Love Dwells in The Single Parent's Home

At times, in the life of families there are serious situations in which spouses cannot stay together for their safety or the safety of their children. Such break ups are tragic but necessary. These separations do not cause God who is Love to depart from your home. He is there is a special way because of your baptism. He is there to guide you and help you. You, the single parent become the primary image of God's love in your children's lives. God's love is manifested in your caring for them, in your attitude toward the people in your life, and also in the way you speak to them about their absent parent. This is an imperfect situation, but not uncommon. Each parent must do their best to provide the safety and security that the children need to grow healthy. The single parents can find comfort and strength for their life's journey in the sacraments of the Church, and the support of their family, friends and their faith community. Jesus is always with you. Jesus reassured all families: "For where two or three are gathered together in my name, there am I in the midst of them." (Mt. 18:20)

————

Whether you are a happy couple, a struggling one, or a single parent, never forget that God is next to you and is present in your home. The sacraments of the Church are the source of many graces that can help you grow in your ability to love and become better icons of God's love to your children. Make your faith your point of reference, like the North Star is to voyagers at sea and let the wisdom of the Scripture and of the Catholic tradition guide you. "Christ dwells with [you], gives [you] the strength to take up [your] crosses and to follow him, to rise again after [you] have fallen, to forgive one another, to bear one another's burdens," (Catechism of the Catholic Church 1642).

Reflection:

- If you could see Jesus next to you in your home, how differently would you act or speak toward the members of your family?
- What is the common ground, the point of reference that holds you and your spouse together?

Action:

Whether you are a co-parent or a single parent, you know that reflection and conversation are good, but without action, little progress is made in a family. As you conclude this chapter, you are encouraged to make a simple resolution. Agree with your family members on one small action that you will take as a result of having read this chapter. When choosing your action, consider the suggestions below, and encourage other ideas from members of your family. Keep it easy and simple!

Write your plan here:

_____

I encourage you to track your family's journey as suggested on page 12 of the Introduction.

Suggestions:

1. Talk to your children about their baptism, and mark the date on the family calendar.
2. Talk to your children about your wedding, and show them pictures. Explain why your wedding was special.
3. Give the Bible a prominent place in your home and read to your children stories from the Bible and books about the lives of the saints.
4. Ensure that your children are familiar with the basic prayers used in our Catholic tradition. Find some of these in the Appendix.
5. Start listening to inspirational materials from Catholic podcasts or a Catholic radio station available in your area, either over the air or online, such as www.relevantradio.com, or www.ewtn.com, or www.catholictv.org.
6. Ensure that each room in your home is decorated with a crucifix or a holy image.

Conversation Starters for Families

Below are topics for conversation with your children on the subject of God's presence in your home. You, as a parent or a grandparent, can bring these subjects up during informal chats at home, during car rides, or during meals. Use the questions below as conversation starters. Word them in a way that is appropriate for each child's age.

1. "Why do we go to church? Why is church a special place?"
2. "What are some special churches we have visited?
3. "What in our home reminds you of God?"
4. "What is your favorite image or statue of Jesus?"
5. "What are some of the ways you express your love for your brothers and sisters?"
6. "If you could see Jesus in our home, what would you say to him, and what would you do differently when you play with your friends?"
7. Explain to your children that God is love, and when they feel loved by someone, it is God touching them with his goodness.
8. Tell your children: "Remember that whenever I give you a hug it is as if Jesus gave you a hug."
9. If you are a single parent, tell the child that you love them, and remind them that the absent parent loves them too.
10. If a parent is not Catholic, encourage them to share memories of their family's religious sense in their childhood home.

Conversation Starters for Parents or Groups

<u>Notes for the group leader:</u>
-Begin the meeting with the prayer to the Holy Family (end of Chapter 1).
-Start the conversation with a general question, such as: what did you find interesting and helpful in this chapter? What story touched you the most? What anecdotes or situations from your own life came to mind as you read the chapter?
-Continue the conversation by using the questions below.
-Close the meeting by asking participants to identify one thing they want to remember from the chapter or from the conversation that just took place.

1. What are some of the sacred places in your community that you find most inspiring?
2. How was your experience of home life when you were growing up? What role did faith play?
3. If I walked with you through your home right now, what would I see and hear that tells me that I am in a Catholic home?
4. What do you have in your home that reminds you and your children of God's presence?
5. Home is where we are touched by Love. Can you recall any particular situation in your childhood when you felt loved?
6. The author writes that your home is God's workshop. What does that mean to you?
7. What do you know or remember about your Baptism?
8. What do you remember about your wedding?
9. Pope Francis says that couples are "Living icons of God's love." What does that mean to you?
10. What would a non-Catholic parent tell his children about their own faith journey?

Prayer:

A Parent's Prayer, found at the end of Chapter 1, or the **Prayer to the Holy Family** found in the Appendix.

CHAPTER 3

HOME IS A SCHOOL OF PRAYER

A Father's Blessing

A friend of ours, Mickey, shared the following personal story. "As a young parent, I learned to bless my children during a men's retreat. Each evening, after night prayers, I would trace the sign of the cross with my thumb on each son's forehead saying, 'May almighty God bless you in the name of the Father, and of the Son, and of the Holy Spirit, with life everlasting. Amen.' After the blessing, I would give my two sons a little pinch on their noses. That was the signal that the day was done.

"One evening, my oldest, who was about twelve, looked up at me with a challenging expression on his face and said, 'Dad, I don't need your blessing anymore!' I was taken aback by this declaration. I hesitated for a moment, and then as I started responding, I was interrupted by the voice of my younger son, coming from the other bedroom, who yelled, 'Yea, dad, I don't need it either!' I realized that the older was about to step into a new world, which he needed to figure out, and the younger sibling wanted to be as cool as his big brother. I was disappointed, but I obliged them. So, I stopped blessing them openly with the sign of the cross, but I told them that each evening whenever I said "goodnight" to them, it was my blessing for them, and they could not dodge it."

Mickey continued: "Years later, the older decided to go to Officer Candidate School with the Marines. When the day of his departure arrived, the family accompanied him to the airport. As the time approached for boarding the plane, my son turned to me and said, 'Dad, could I have your blessing?' I was touched by this request because it had a lot of meaning for both of us and also because I thought this childhood ritual had been forgotten. I gladly obliged him. A few years later, when the younger decided to walk the Appalachian Trail, a feat that would take him months, he came to me and asked, 'Dad, could I please have your blessing?'"

Whatever prayer ritual parents institute in their home with their young children is likely to remain meaningful to them for the rest of their lives, and it will possibly be passed on to the next generation as a dear expression of faith. Today Mickey's sons are also in the habit of blessing their own children at bedtime. Mickey has now passed, and this daily blessing remains part of his spiritual legacy to the family.

Pope Francis emphasized the importance of parental blessings: "What can be more beautiful than for a father and mother to bless their children at the beginning and end of each day, to trace on their forehead the sign of the cross, as they did on the day of their baptism? Is this not the simplest prayer which parents can offer for their children?" (12-27-2015).

Throughout this book, you will read anecdotes that reflect certain faith practices and prayer traditions. I am not suggesting that you should follow these. Each family is different. I hope that the real-life stories you read prompt you to reflect on how your family prays and practices the Catholic faith. It is up to you to create the prayer rituals that best fit your family's life style.

Reflection:

- What are some of your childhood memories of prayer in your home?
- What prayers do you pray most often with your family today?
- What do you think about the practice of blessing your children?

Your Home Is a Domestic Church

I learned about Jesus, Mary, the angels, and the saints in my childhood home. It is there that I first prayed. It is there that I learned about my Christian faith and its practice; about what is right and what is wrong, and it is there that my conscience started to be formed. From my family, I acquired an outlook on life that is full of hope because it includes faith. When God is part of the picture, we cannot despair; there is always hope. In retrospect, looking back at my life, as if in a rear-view mirror, I realize that during those formative years, my home was my church, the primary place where I learned to pray, was evangelized, catechized, and prepared to participate in the life of the Church and of society.

St. John Paul II, On October 6, 1995, during his visit to the United States, spoke about the family as a "domestic church." During his homily at the Aqueduct Racetrack in Brooklyn, NY, he said, "Catholic parents must learn to form their family as a 'domestic Church,' a church in the home as it were, where God is honored, his law is respected, prayer is a normal event, virtue is transmitted by word and example, and everyone shares the hopes, the problems and sufferings of everyone else."

The title of "domestic church," used to describe the Christian family, is something relatively new in the language of the Church. It first appeared in the documents of the Second Vatican Council in the 1960s and has since been used more frequently by all the popes. Pope Francis gave a definition of Church that helps us understand how our home is a domestic church. He called the universal Church the family of families (AL 87). Your family is a small unit of that universal family that is the Church. Your family is a piece of the Church, the church in your home, the domestic church. You, the parents, are the leaders (the shepherds) of this small unit of the universal church. Your mission, because of your baptism, is to lead the family in prayer, teach the faith, and seek its wellbeing. Your parish community is there to help you tend to your family's spiritual needs. St. John Paul II and the popes after him have repeatedly said that the future of society and of the Church depends on the health of the family. Your Christian family is church, the church in your home.

Reflection:

- How was your faith passed on to you?
- What are your children's favorite Bible stories?
- How is your family active in your parish today?

Your Home Is a Cradle of the Church

Think for a moment at the home of your childhood. There, within your family, is where your life began; where you were nursed, nurtured, and cared for. It is there that you learned who you are, your identity, the place where you belong. You were given a name, introduced to a clan, and slowly you started thinking, acting, believing and hopefully praying like the people around you. The memories, good or bad, of those early experiences of family life will remain with you for the rest of your life.

Today, it is up to you to create a home environment for your children—a place where your faith can be passed on to them, it can blossom and will be a permanent part of their lives even if they were to choose to temporarily ignore it.

Do you remember the baptism of your children? At the beginning of the rite, the celebrant addressed you and said, "You have asked to have this child baptized. In doing so, you are accepting the responsibility of training him/her in the practice of the faith." Then he added, "Do you clearly understand what you are undertaking?" And, you replied: "We do." With that you accepted your mandate as Catholic Parents to teach and bear witness to the faith to your children by what you do and say.

What you undertook at the baptism of your children is an awesome responsibility! That may feel overwhelming, but you are not alone. The Church gave you godparents to help you, and of course, the whole Catholic community is standing by to support your efforts.

Children learn by doing what their parents do. Your children will learn from you, even when you do not intend to teach them. When our daughters were old enough to go out on their own in the evening, Teri started the practice of lighting a candle while they were gone as a prayer to their guardian angel to keep them safe. If they were late coming home, she would write a note that said, "The candle is lit for you. Please blow it out when you get home." Our daughters never commented on this practice, nor about this way of praying. One day, our youngest came home from college unexpectedly, and Teri and I had plans to attend a function with friends that evening. Later that night, when we returned, we found a candle lit with a note, "Mom and Dad, the candle is lit for you. Please, blow it out!"

Reflection:
- Think of one situation that shows how your children mimic what you do.
- What do you do in your home that is intended to help your children grow in faith?
- What role did you ask your children's godparents to play, or what role do you wish they would play?

Your Home Is the First Place of Worship

When I was growing up, my uncle, who was a missionary priest, taught me to always write at the end of my homework the letters AMDG. AMDG is the abbreviation of the Latin words: Ad Majorem Dei Gloria. He explained that the letters stand for the Latin words that mean "for the greater glory of God." He explained to me that everything I do, whether it is playing soccer, running, or doing homework, I should always do it in a way that pleases and honors God. The lesson I learned was that we are here to serve God and to give him glory with our life. We strive to make him proud of us in everything we do. We are his creation; his children.

Our life, with its ups and downs, when it is offered to God in a spirit of service to him, is an act of worship – it is prayer, as St. Paul explains to the Romans, "I appeal to you, therefore, brethren, to present your bodies as a living sacrifice, holy and acceptable to God, which is your spiritual worship" (Rom. 12:1). That is what we are to do in our Catholic home. We worship God through our daily routines. So, cooking meals, changing diapers, making beds, going to work, taking care of the car, mowing the lawn, teaching our children and playing with them, and all the other chores and responsibilities of our life are sacred work – they are the liturgy of our domestic church. When we do these with the intention of serving God by following his will, we honor and worship him and grow in holiness. The path to holiness for the Christian family is to live in God's presence with an attitude of service to him.

St. Basil the Great wrote: "This is how you pray continually – by joining yourself to God through your whole way of life, so that your life becomes one continuous and uninterrupted prayer."

Reflection:
- If you could see Jesus next to you while you are doing your daily chores how would you do them differently?
- How would you tell your children that when they do their chores or homework, they should do them in a manner that pleases God?
- What were the first prayers you learned as a child?

Prayer Rituals of the Catholic Home
Since love is the essence of home life, and a family's home life

is the liturgy of their domestic church, one important aspect of this liturgy is the practice of rituals that promote love. I call these "Love Rituals." Every home has two main groups of love rituals: love rituals of interaction with God, we call these prayers, and love rituals of interaction among family members. Through these two types of love rituals, we grow in love with God and with one another. The two groups are inseparable. We cannot love God and ignore the needs of the members of our family. This chapter will address the first group of love rituals: the prayer rituals of the domestic church; the next will address the second: the love rituals that build up and sustain family relationships in your domestic church.

The Christian home, like the Church, needs prayer rituals. These are prayers that are special to us and we recite them regularly as a family, when possible. Among these are devotional prayers such as the Morning Offering, the prayers before meals, or bedtime prayers, or the recitation of the rosary, or saying the Chaplet of Divine Mercy, or a simple prayer for a saint's intercession in a moment of need, or a blessing of the children before bedtime. These prayers are sources of strength in moments of fear and anxiety, and vehicles for thanking God for our life's blessings.

God is a member of our family and talking to him as a family about what is going on can be very helpful. "The family that prays together stays together" is a saying made popular by Venerable Father Peyton. Today, science is proving that this saying is true. Researchers are finding that couples who practice their faith regularly are more satisfied with their marriage.

Pope Francis emphasizes the important role that mothers play in teaching children to pray and in passing on the faith. He writes: "Mothers often communicate the deepest meaning of religious practice in the first prayers and acts of devotion that their children learn... Without mothers, not only would there be no new faithful, but the faith itself would lose a good part of its simple and profound warmth..." (AL 318).

Prayer sustains us in the most difficult moments. In 2020, in the middle of the COVID-19 pandemic, my father-in-law's health deteriorated, and we were not allowed to visit him. He did not contract COVID, but he was very ill. This isolation was distressing to him and to all the members of the family. Then his condition worsened and he was placed in hospice care. It was at this point that my father-in-law asked his children and grandchildren to help him prepare for his final passage by praying with him, "Would you pray with me each day?" A member of the family suggested that we should say the rosary with him each day at 1:30 pm. That was a convenient time for him.

And so, a new prayer ritual was started in our family. Each day, we would connect via Zoom with my father-in-law to recite the rosary. This was an experience that lasted six months until he died. And even on his last day, when he could no longer speak but could hear us, we prayed the rosary in his presence. Reciting the rosary with us each day became the highlight of his days while in isolation. On the other hand, this experience of prayer as a family, during a difficult time, even if it was via Zoom, allowed all the family members who are scattered across the country to reconnect spiritually with one another. Mary was with us, protecting us under her maternal mantle as we walked with our patriarch to the next life. Pope Francis is right. He told his audience on November 4, 2020, that prayer has the power to transform into something good even the drudgeries and the unpleasant aspects of life.

Reflection:

- What are the moments in your daily life when you need God's grace the most?
- What are the prayer rituals of your domestic church—the prayers that you say more often as a family?

Sacramentals—Tools for Prayer

In our Catholic tradition, we use blessed objects to decorate our home as a reminder of God's presence and as tools for prayer. The religious articles and artifacts Catholics display in their homes are not idols. They are reminders of the presence of God and of the spiritual family of angels and saints that surrounds us and cares about us. Among these religious articles are images of Jesus, Mary and the saints, the crucifix, holy water, rosary beads, the Bible, and many others. The Catholic Church calls these "sacramentals" because they "are sacred signs which bear a resemblance to the sacraments" (Catechism of the Catholic Church 1667). They are sources of grace.

Other sacramentals are prayers, such as the sign of the cross, the recitation of the rosary, a prayer before meals, and others.

A fond childhood memory takes me back to a time when my family recited the rosary during the month of October. In the Catholic Church, October is the month when we celebrate the feast of Our Lady of the Rosary, which is on October 7. During this month, after dinner, all the members of my family--my parents, my sister, my brother, my grandparents--and I would gather in the kitchen where we had the only wood-burning stove for cooking and for heating our apartment. Up on the wall, in a corner over the sink, was a small statue of the Sacred Heart. In front of it, a light burned day and night. Our family had a strong devotion to Mary and to the Sacred Heart. Kneeling on our chairs, we turned toward the Sacred Heart, and we prayed the rosary.

My childhood memory of that moment is not so much about the experience of praying the rosary but about what was going on while our family prayed. My grandfather was sitting by the stove reciting the rosary while roasting chestnuts. The experience of my family united in prayer combined with the scent of roasted chestnuts has remained with me to this day. As a child, I always looked forward to eating the roasted chestnuts with my family after the rosary. And, to this day, the scent of roasted chestnuts is a reminder of the days when I said the rosary with my parents.

Today, that same statue of the Sacred Heart in front of which my family prayed sits in our home, here in the United States. The effigy belonged to my grandmother until she died. It was a gift from my uncle to her on the occasion of our family's consecration to the Sacred Heart, just before World War II. When my grandmother died, she left the statue to my father, and when my father moved to a nursing home, the Sacred Heart moved with him. After my father's death, my siblings gave the statue to Teri and me to be placed in our home in the United States. Today, the statue of the Sacred Heart owned by my family for over 80 years remains for us an invitation to daily prayer.

"The various expressions of popular piety are a treasure of spirituality for many families," writes Pope Francis (AL 318).

Reflection:

- Which of the following do you find in your home?

Crosses and Crucifix,	Holy water,	Scapular
Statues, Images,	Blessed Candles,	Holy Bible
Blessed Oils,	Blessed Palms,	Relics
Prayer Cards,	Rosary Beads,	Medals

- What Catholic prayer rituals do you want to pass on to your children?

We Are Not Alone

As Christians, we know that we do not travel our life's journey alone. We are accompanied by angels and saints. In the books of Tobit in the Old Testament, we read about Tobiah, a young man who was sent by his father on a journey to a strange land. Since he did not know how to reach the destination, he searched and found a trusted companion, Raphael. Tobiah did not know that Raphael was an angel. Tobiah's journey was successful because he trusted Raphael and listened to his advice. We are all accompanied by our guardian angel.

When we were baptized, we became members of God's family. The Catholic Church calls this family the Communion of Saints. God's family includes those who are already in heaven, the angels, and the saints, those who have died and are being purified, and the rest of us who are on a journey to holiness. At baptism, we became members of this body of saints, and our life on Earth is dedicated to celebrating the goodness of God in union with Christ and all the saints.

As members of the family of saints, we help one another. We pray for the dead who are undergoing purification, and we turn to the saints in heaven, asking them to intercede and pray for us in our moments of need, and they do.

Parents often turn to saints for spiritual help and guidance for their children. Catholic families for centuries have named their children after Mary, St. Joseph, St. Anthony, and other saints to give each child a model of holiness and to invoke the saint's protection over the child.

Some families have chosen a saint to be their family's patron, someone who intercedes for them when special graces are needed. For example, Teri's grandparents chose St. Catherine of Siena for their family's patron saint. Each day, they ended their blessing before a meal with these words, "Jesus, Mary and Joseph pray for us. St. Catherine pray for us." Later, Teri's parents chose as the patron saint for their family St. Martin de Porres. In their home, the blessing before each meal ended with, "Jesus, Mary and Joseph pray for us. St. Martin, pray for us." Each of the six children and their respective families scattered across the country has learned to pray to St. Martin whenever facing some difficulties. Over the years, it has become a legend among the members of the clan that when we pray a novena to St. Martin, the saint may send a sign to indicate that he is listening. The sign is often the sighting of a mouse. In his lifetime, St. Martin was a Dominican brother of mixed race. Because of this, he was given a lower status in the community and assigned menial roles. According to the legend, the saint was known for having been kind to everyone, including animals, among these the mice that had infested his monastery.

I want to close with a personal anecdote. Years ago, I was being considered for a job in a different city. The job would have meant a significant promotion and a blessing for our family. In anticipation for the interview, our family started a novena to St. Martin. The day before the interview, Teri and my youngest daughter drove me to the airport, which was about one hour away from our home. Later that evening, at about the time when my plane was to land at my destination, while they were driving home, a mouse crossed the road in front of their car. Both Teri and my daughter saw it and were shocked. That evening Teri called me at my hotel and said, "You got the job! We saw a mouse today." The next day I went to the interview, and a few weeks later, I was made an offer. In our extended family, it has become common that whenever someone sees a mouse, we ask one another: "Has anyone been praying to St. Martin?" Never doubt the power of prayer! Mary and the saints are our friends.

Praying to the saints asking for their intercession is not something magical. We do not always get what we ask. We pray with the understanding that God will grant what is best for us. In his generosity, he is wiser than us and gives us what we truly need. A priest friend of mine likes to say, "God is not a vending machine!"

Pope Francis himself has a great devotion to St. Thérèse of Lisieux. He has said repeatedly that when he has a problem, he turns to St. Thérèse for her intercession. He explained that he entrusts the problem to her. He doesn't ask her to resolve it, but to take it into her hands and to help him. He added, "Almost always, I receive a rose as a sign."

Reflection:

- Does your family have a patron saint? Who is it?
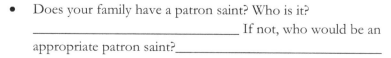
 _____ If not, who would be an appropriate patron saint?_____

- Are your children named after a saint? If not, what would be the appropriate saint's name for each of your children?

Praying With the Communion of Saints

The private prayers said in your home and the many sacrifices you make for the good of your family are important for your salvation. They are part of the liturgy of your domestic church. But that private prayer cannot remain isolated. God calls us as a people and saves us as a people. As a family, a domestic church, we are an integral part of something greater than us: the Communion of Saints. We need to worship God - Father, Son, and Holy Spirit - with the community of the Church in union with all the saints in heaven. Worshiping as a people is part of our duty toward God. This is why the Catholic Church asks us to attend Mass every Sunday and on days of obligation. Pope Francis reminds us that "The family's communal journey of prayer culminates by sharing together in the Eucharist" (AL 318).

It is in the Mass and the sacraments that we encounter Christ. When we participate in the Mass, we unite the prayers and the sacrifices of our domestic church to the sacrifice of Christ and, through the power of the Holy Spirit, we offer them to the Father in thanksgiving for our redemption.

Your family's participation in the Mass and the reception of the Eucharist, especially on Sundays, is a moment of family renewal. Again, Pope Francis writes, "Jesus knocks at the door of families, to share with them the Eucharistic supper... For the food of the Eucharist offers the spouses the strength and incentive needed to live the marriage covenant each day as a 'domestic church'"(AL 318).

Participation in the Mass fills us with the graces we need to go home and continue on our journey toward holiness. Our personal prayers, as wonderful as they may be, need to be grounded in the mysteries of our faith that we celebrate together as a community of believers in the liturgy of the Universal Church.

Reflection:

- What are some of the hardest sacrifices that you make each day for your marriage and your family?
- What is your habit of Mass attendance?
- What aspect of your life do you want to take to the altar on Sunday?

Action:

Whether you are a co-parent or a single parent, you know that reflection and conversation are good, but without action, little progress is made in a family. Hopefully, this chapter has helped you realize that your home life is a path to heaven; and your family is a domestic church. As in previous chapters, I encourage you to choose one very small action that you can take in the coming days to guide your family to grow in faith. When choosing your action, consider the suggestions below and encourage other ideas from members of your family. Keep it easy and simple!

Write your plan here:

_____

_____

I encourage you to track your family's journey as suggested on page 12 of the Introduction.

Suggestions:

1. If you have not done so after reading Chapter 2, ensure that each room of your home has a crucifix or a holy image.
2. Make sure that your children know the following prayers: The Sign of the Cross, the Our Father, the Hail Mary, the Glory Be, and others depending on your children's age.
3. Establish with your children a habit of praying regularly, such as before meals, upon rising, or going to bed, or any other time appropriate for your family.
4. Choose a time during the day or week when you read Bible stories to your children.
5. Explain to your children why we pray and how to pray.
6. Teach your children the prayer to their Guardian Angel. Find the prayer in the Appendix.
7. Explain to your children why we go to Mass and what happens at Mass.
8. Purchase books for your children on the lives of the saints, and read them as bedtime stories.

Conversation Starters for Families

Below are topics for conversation with your children on the subject of prayer. You, as a parent or a grandparent, can bring these subjects up during informal chats at home, during car rides, or during meals. Use the questions below as conversation starters. Word them in a way that is appropriate for each child's age.

1. Ask your child: Do you ever talk to God?
2. What does God say to you when you listen?
3. What are your favorite prayers?
4. If a child has a Christian name, the name of a saint, explain why it was given to them. Give the child that carries a saint's name some information about the saint. If a child does not have a Christian name, ask your child to choose a patron saint to be their intercessor. To help, you can provide them a list.
5. Explain to your children that angels and saints are our friends. We all belong to the same family: God's family.
6. Talk to the child about their guardian angel.
7. Explain to your children why we go to Mass and what happens during Mass.
8. If your family has prayer traditions that have been passed on to you, explain to your children why you do them and what they mean to you.
9. Tell your child that we are all to do everything as best as possible to serve and honor to God, and explain what that means with words the child can understand.
10. If one of the parents is not Catholic, encourage them to share with the children how they prayed in their home when growing up.

Conversation Starters for Parents or Groups

Notes for the group leader:

-Begin the meeting with the prayer to the Holy Family (end of Chapter 1).

-Start the conversation with a general question, such as: what did you find interesting and helpful in this chapter? What story touched you the most? What anecdotes or situations from your own life came to mind as you read the chapter?

-Continue the conversation by using the questions below.

-Close the meeting by asking participants to identify one thing they want to remember from the chapter or from the conversation that just took place.

1. What are your thoughts about the practice of blessing your children?

2. How have you noticed your children following your example— mimicking you? Share some instances.

3. What were the first prayers you learned as a child?

4. What prayers are most common in your home?

5. Where is your family Bible kept in your home, and when do you read from it?

6. What are your children's favorite Bible stories?

7. How often does your family participate at Mass?

8. What do you think about having a patron saint for your family? If so, who might that be?

9. Are your children named after saints? If not, which saint would be an appropriate model and protector for each of them?

10. If a member of the group is practicing a different faith, invite them to share the typical forms of home prayers and community prayer in their tradition.

Prayer:

A Parent's Prayer, found at the end of Chapter 1, or the **Prayer to the Holy Family** found in the Appendix.

CHAPTER 4

HOME IS AN APPRENTICESHIP TO LOVING

Love

St. John Paul II, in his Apostolic Exhortation on the Family, reminds us that we are made for love. "Love is the fundamental and innate vocation of every human person" because God created us in his own image. (FC 11). God is love, and his is love permeates all of creation. The warmth of God's tenderness is felt in the affection, the kindness, the generosity and self-giving we experience in our family relationships. Family love contains a spark of divine love, writes Pope Francis (AL 172), and St. John Paul II adds that the family is a community of life and love willed by God (FC 11). Life in the family is an apprenticeship to loving.

But what is love? We may think of love as a feeling, but ultimately for love to truly be love, it needs to be expressed in words and actions that benefit another person. St. Thomas Aquinas writes that to love is to will the good of the other person; to do what is best for them.

Can you remember a time when a stranger did you a favor—

something you did not expect, and it was exactly what you needed?

I landed at the Paris Charles de Gaulle Airport in the early afternoon, and my flight to the United States did not leave until the following morning. After checking in at the airport hotel, I decided that I had time to go to the center of Paris to walk the Champs-Élysées from the Arc de Triomphe to the Louvre. To avoid an expensive taxi ride, I opted to take the local public transportation. I boarded a bus at the airport that would take me to the nearest subway station. At my stop, I stepped off the bus and looked around for the entrance to the station. To my surprise, I did not see a subway sign anywhere near me. I panicked because I feared I had chosen the wrong stop, and the bus had already left. I did not know where I was, and worse of all, my knowledge of the French language was limited.

As I stood on the sidewalk, feeling uncertain and confused, I felt someone tapping my shoulder. An older gentleman said to me in French, "Do you need help?" I replied as best as I could that I was looking for the subway station. He smiled, grabbed my arm, and said in English with a strong accent, "I will take you. Follow me." We walked in silence for about two blocks, and then he pointed to the entrance of the subway. I was relieved and very grateful. I thanked him, and he went on his way.

Perhaps you have had a similar experience of getting lost in a city unfamiliar to you. What this stranger did for me was truly a generous act. He could have just given me directions in French and then left, and I would have probably forgotten them or not understood them. Instead, he went out of his way to take me where I wanted to go. He walked with me to make sure I arrived at my destination. That was an act of love. He did what was best for me at that moment.

Pope Francis reminded us of what love is in his Lenten message for 2021. "Love rejoices in seeing others grow. Hence, it suffers when others are anguished, lonely, sick, homeless, despised, or in need. Love is a leap of the heart; it brings us out of ourselves and creates bonds of sharing and communion."

One day, when I was five, my father asked me to go with him for a ride on his bicycle. I remember that I was not feeling well, but for me going out on my father's bicycle was a treat. Eventually, our excursion took us to the hospital under the pretext that my father needed to visit a friend. I was quickly diagnosed with a case of scarlet fever, a bacterial infection that at the time was considered a serious childhood illness because antibiotics were not available. I was kept in the hospital and was confined to a room for several weeks. My only companion was my grandmother, who was with me day and night during that time. I could not have visitors, and my only contact with my family was through a window overlooking the street. In the evenings, my parents and my siblings would come to a particular spot on the street and wave at me. What stands out in my memory of that long stay in the hospital is not the discomfort I felt but the love of my grandmother, Margherita. I have never forgotten what she did for me. She put her life on hold to be quarantined with me day and night for one month. She stood by my side, held me when my fever was high, calmed me down when I refused the daily injections. She entertained me when I was bored; she sang to me; she read to me; she told stories. She was my guardian angel during my isolation. In her presence, I experienced love, which for me at the time was affection, tenderness, and security. These were the things I needed the most.

Reflection:
- When was the last time someone surprised you with an unexpected act of kindness?
- How would you define love in your own words? Love is...

The Importance of Good Habits

The love of my grandmother and of the stranger who helped me in Paris are wonderful acts of kindness. They are love, but the love that we need in our homes has to be more than just a collection of occasional acts of kindness. Our home life as a family needs to be held together by a pattern of daily habits forming a lifestyle – a way of interacting through which we repeatedly express our love, unity, and commitment to one another. For our family to thrive, we need habits that help us say to one another over and over: we are one even when we argue and disagree, we care for one another even if sometimes we cause each other pain, we are all connected even if sometimes it does not feel like we are, and we stand by one another during difficult times no matter how hard it is. Then, loving becomes our way of being as a family.

I remember a phone call that Teri and I had with her mother, Jerry, in her last days before she passed. The conversation was a rambling of random thoughts linked by a common refrain, "Stay connected." "Stay connected" was the message that Jerry preached to the whole family before she died. Everyone still seems to remember it.

Staying connected as a family and being united are not achieved through random acts of kindness. They are achieved by creating habits that express our love for one another. Habits are behaviors that we repeat almost without thinking. Psychologists tell us that our habits shape our lives. Gretchen Rubin writes in her book *Better Than Before*, "Habits are the invisible architecture of our daily life. We repeat about 40% of our behavior almost daily, so our habits shape our existence and our future." Your children's lives are shaped by the habits they learn today in your home, following your example and guidance.

Reflection:
- What are some of the good habits you learned from your parents?
- What are some of the habits you want to pass on to your children?

Love Rituals
In the previous chapter, we reflected on the prayer ritual of the domestic church. In this chapter, we are considering the love rituals, the loving interactions which create, build up and hold together the

faith community that lives in your home. Both types of rituals help us serve God. "prayer rituals" help us grow in love with God, and "love rituals" help us grow in love with the people God put in our life as our family.

One of these love rituals is the habit of welcoming and acknowledging one another. When I was a child, my father worked at the local manufacturing plant in our small town. He would go to work each morning at 8:00 am and come home at 6:00 pm when the plant sounded a loud horn announcing the end of the work day. The whole town could hear the sound. To us children, who were playing with our friends, the sound of the horn was the signal that it was time to go home. At the house, we would find our mother looking out of the kitchen window, waiting for my father to arrive. As she spotted him approaching on his bicycle, she would gather us and tell us, "Go to the door to welcome and greet your father!"

That was an expression of love ritualized in a daily "Welcome home!" to my father. My father was always glad to see us. He would hug us, and then he would walk over to my mother to give her a kiss.

What I learned from my mother was the importance of acknowledging a member of the family returning home, especially after a long day at work or after having been away for a while. The daily love ritual of greeting my father or anyone coming to visit became a habit that has remained with me to this day. Whenever Teri returns home from some activity, I greet her and welcome her home. I know that she appreciates the gesture because she has started doing the same for me, and believe me, it feels good to be greeted kindly after a hard day at work, or when returning from a trip.

A friend of mine wrote to me, "Greeting my husband when he comes home from work has been a practice I have followed 'religiously' for all these years. Someone suggested it early in our marriage and I try to do it faithfully—when I neglect to stop and make time to greet him, it feels like sin."

What happens in your home when you return from work or from the store? Does anyone besides your dog notice that you have been gone and have now returned? If it seems that no one notices, you could incorrectly conclude that no one cares. That may not be accurate. Perhaps the members of your family care a lot about you, but no one told them how disheartened you feel when you walk into the house after a long day at work and no one acknowledges that you are back, or how confusing it is when a member of your family leaves the house and no one knows that they have gone or when they will return. A friend shared that one day she was at home working in the kitchen while thinking that her husband was upstairs working on a project. As time passed, after a few hours, she went to check on him and found that he was not there. He had left the house without telling her. She did not know where he was nor when he would return. She felt hurt and decided to speak to him about the incident when he came back.

In our families, we need predictability and accountability – we need stability. This is achieved by forming habits and routines that tell the members of our clan that we are connected and united as a family even when we are apart, or we disagree; that we belong to one another and are accountable. These habits define the culture of our family and form traditions that will be carried on for generations.

When I traveled extensively for business, I was always happy when, upon reaching my destination, I would find a note from Teri in my suitcase wishing me a successful trip. That was a love ritual. Even from a distance, that note and gesture kept us connected. Parents and children stay connected during the day with notes in the lunchbox, or a surprise treat. Some couples stay connected through text messages or phone calls during the day. Others do so by getting together, from time to time for lunch or a cup of coffee, and of course, by keeping up the practice of regular date nights.

Reflection:

- What do you think of the ritual of greeting your spouse and family members as they come home? How can your family do better at doing this?
- What are some of the daily habits that help you stay connected with the members of your family even when you are apart?

Love Rituals Are Necessary to Keep the Family Strong

Pope Francis gives us some examples of love rituals that keep family relationship strong. He writes, "Young married couples should be encouraged to develop a routine that gives a healthy sense of closeness and stability through shared daily rituals. These could include a morning kiss, an evening blessing, waiting at the door to welcome each other home, taking trips together, and sharing household chores" (AL 226). These daily love rituals form a structure in the life of your family that makes your home the place where love resides, and life in your home becomes an apprenticeship to loving for all the members.

Every family needs to have love rituals to maintain healthy relationships. The love rituals of your Catholic home are in many ways similar to the love ritual of any other family in your neighborhood. For example, most families have ways of greeting one another, staying connected, spending time together, and caring for the needs of the members of the family, and many others. One unique ingredient that is found in the Catholic home is the Christian faith. Faith motivates and guides family members in practicing these love rituals because it gives meaning and purpose to what we do. Faith also gives us Jesus as the model for loving. Jesus said to his disciples at the Last Supper: "This is my commandment: love one another as I love you." (Jn. 15:12). In addition, the practice of the faith, through the participation in the sacraments, gives the members of the family access to the divine graces which help them grow in the way they love.

How is Jesus the model for our family? We learn about Jesus' way of loving from the pages of the Gospels. In addition, today, Christ is also our model through the way he loves his Bride, the Church. He does so most concretely in the seven sacraments: Baptism, Confirmation, Eucharist, Penance, Anointing of the Sick, Holy Orders and Matrimony. The love of Christ that sustains his Church through the rituals of the seven sacraments is the blueprint and model for the love rituals that sustain our family, our domestic church.

The Rituals of the Universal Church Are a Blueprint for the Rituals of the Catholic Home

The Catholic Church divides the seven sacraments into three groups based on the graces Christ gives his Church: Sacraments of Initiation, Sacraments of Healing and Sacraments at the Service of Communion.

1. In the sacraments of Initiation: Baptism, Confirmation, and the Eucharist, Christ, through the Holy Spirit, connects us to the life of the Trinity and helps us build and maintain a relationship with the Father. In Baptism he cleanses us and welcomes us into his Father's family. In Confirmation he binds us more perfectly to himself and to the Church, and strengthens us with the gifts of the Holy Spirit. In the Eucharist, he gathers us as a community to celebrate the memorial of his death and resurrection, and to nourish us with his body and blood.

2. In the sacraments of Healing: Penance and Anointing of the Sick, Christ forgives and heals us. Through Penance he absolves our sins and restores our relationship with the Father and with the community of the Church. And through the Anointing of the Sick, he heals us spiritually and comforts us during moments of physical pain.

3. In the sacraments at the Service of Communion: Holy Orders and Matrimony, Christ calls us to join him in serving his Bride, the Church by embracing the vocations to the priesthood or to marriage. These sacraments consecrate us to serving God through a personal calling that enriches and sustains the community of believers.

As Christ keeps the Universal Church alive and growing

through the rituals of the seven sacraments, our family, the domestic church, can look to these sacraments as a blueprint for creating love rituals, good habits, that will help our family grow in unity and love.

Let's explore three groups of family love rituals that parallel the sacraments:

1) **The love rituals that connect and build up our family's communion.** These keep us connected in our family relationships in a similar way that the Sacraments of Initiation, through Christ and the Holy Spirit, bind us to the life of the Trinity.

2) **The love rituals that repair damaged family relationships and comfort us in moments of pain.** These heal our family relationships in a similar way that the Sacraments of Healing, through Christ and the Holy Spirit, repair and restore our relationship with God and the Church.

3) **The love rituals through which our family members serve one another and sustain the life of the family.** Through these we serve our family in a similar way that the Christ and the Holy Spirit through Sacraments of Service, serve the Church and the Father.

1. Love Rituals that Connect and Create Communion—These rituals are habits: actions, words and celebrations through which we welcome one another, bond together as a family, and celebrate our unity. They help us feel that we belong.

A very important love ritual that bonds family members and celebrates our unity is the family meal; a meal where all members, or as many as possible, are together daily, or several times a week, or weekly. Nancy Gibbs in an article published by TIME/CNN (June 2006) describes what happens around the family dinner table with these words: "This is where the tribe comes to transmit wisdom, embedded expectations, confess, forgive and repair."

In contemporary society, having a daily family meal has become more difficult because school, work schedules, social commitments and other activities are pulling family members in different directions. There is also limited time for meal preparation. It is far easier to let members of the family grab something to eat on the way to their activity, or to serve pizza and let everyone grab a slice, and eat while watching TV.

When Teri and I got married we brought to our relationship our individual routines for eating. We started by watching the news on TV while eating dinner together. We thought it was an efficient way to use our time. That was the habit I had developed when I was single. Soon, however, we agreed that eating while watching TV was not good for us. What we really wanted was to eat together in each other's company. Therefore, we decided to turn off the TV during our meals, even if we did not have anything to talk about.

When our children were young, family dinner became a very important moment in our day. I have to admit that in those days, life was also less complicated. Teri worked part time and I had a private practice as a marriage and family counselor and my schedule varied from day to day. Some days I was free in the early afternoon, and we had dinner at our regular time, generally around 6:00 pm. On other days, I had to go back to work in the evenings. Teri knew my schedule, so we planned our dinners around my availability. There were days when our dinner was at 4:00 pm and others much later, but we had supper together every day. Our daughters often complained that they could not play with their friends or watch their favorite TV show, and we used the opportunity to restate the importance of eating together.

Family dinners, especially when children are young, can be an experience that a parent would not want to miss. Much happens around the dinner table. At times, our daughters carried on their own conversation during the meal, and by listening to their chatter, we, parents, felt more a part of their lives. We learned what they were thinking; what they were concerned about, their fears, and their dreams.

John Cuddeback, Ph.D., professor of Philosophy at Christendom College writes that eating together is, in and of itself, a life lesson. "At the table we discover that we belong; that life is always shared – we are never alone; that we begin by listening, and that others have something to say; that we too have something to say, and others will listen – because they love us." (Institute for Family Studies, May 11, 2022)

Today it may not be possible for some families to have dinner together every evening. I know a family whose members have breakfast together every day instead of dinner; others have a family meal every Sunday.

There are many findings from recent research that point to the benefits of eating together as a couple and as a family. Robin Fox, an anthropologist who teaches at Rutgers University, says that family dinners engrave the souls: "A meal is about civilizing children. It is about teaching them to be a member of their culture." Teenagers are the ones that seem to benefit the most from regular family meals, although they may be the ones resisting the most. Studies show that the more often families eat together, the less likely teens are to smoke, drink, do drugs, and develop eating disorders, and the more likely they are to do well in school.

During our family meals, it is easy to allow interruptions and distractions caused by the ever-present TV or electronic gadgets. Make your family meal, truly your family meal. Sit down at the table and turn off the TV and other electronic gadgets. Start with a prayer: make the sign of the cross and say a blessing (see Appendix) and then enjoy the food and the company. This is time for your family to be family without distractions! Do not forget to thank and compliment the person who prepared it.

Reflection:

Examples of love rituals that connect and create communion

In reflecting on the presence of these love rituals in the life of your family, ask yourself: what do we do regularly that helps us accept and welcome one another, stay connected, and remember that we belong together?

Read the sample list below, place a check mark by those rituals that remind you of what you already do in your home. Then, add any that you do that are not listed here. Finally, ask yourself: which of our love rituals, such as eating together, or greeting each other, could be improved in our home?

Sample love rituals:

- A morning kiss or hug.
- A welcome home greeting.
- A goodbye kiss.
- A kind word: "Please" when we need a favor. "Can you please help me with…"
- A "thank you" after a favor was received.
- A meal together sitting at the family table (without outside interruptions).
- A hug or a kiss as a recognition of a promise kept.
- A compliment for a job well done. For example, a thank you to the person who prepared the meal.
- A prayer together.
- A family gathering, such as a family vacation, a walk in the park together.
- A birthday or anniversary celebration
- A favorite family game played together.
- A smile to connect at different moments during the day.
- A gentle touch—holding hands when walking together with your spouse.

- A moment of intentional listening without interrupting in order to understand.
- A moment of intimacy.
- A phone call, a note, or a text during the day to stay in touch.

Any others?

2. Rituals that Heal and Give Comfort—These love rituals are interactions through which we reconnect and heal relationships after a disagreement or a misunderstanding. Some examples of these are the habits of saying "I'm sorry. I made a mistake." Or, "I did not realize I was hurting you. Please forgive me." Or, "I did not understand what you meant. Can we please start this conversation over?" "Can we put this conversation on hold for a few minutes? I need to calm down so I can better listen and absorb what you are telling me." They can also be actions, such as a hug, a kiss, a pat on the back, a smile, and many other nonverbal messages that convey repentance and invite reconciliation.

In working with couples, I learned that each marriage has its own different ritual for reconciling after a disagreement. One couple told me that when they are upset with each other, at first, they tend to spend time alone in different rooms, then, as time passes, they get progressively closer, until one of them reaches out with a word or a touch or a joke to restart the conversation. Reconciliation rituals vary from couple to couple, but what is common to all couples is that the healing process takes time, and each person heals at a different pace. Saying "Sorry!" is easy, but for the injured party, it may take longer to put the incident behind and move forward emotionally. Sometimes humor helps.

Teri and I learned early in our marriage that after a disagreement, we seem to heal at different paces. For me, it is easier to put the incident and the hurt aside and move on. However, for Teri, it is more difficult. She needs time. She often reminds me of an incident that happened early in our marriage. One day, after an argument, Teri left the house and went to the shopping center to clear her mind. While at the mall, she stopped to buy a cookie for herself but felt guilty about not buying one for me, so she did. Then she continued her shopping while holding on to the cookie for me. When she returned home, she came to find me and threw the cookie at me and said, "I could not buy a cookie for me without buying one for you!" We both started laughing. That gesture broke the ice. All couples need to learn their ways to reconnect, and in most cases, time is an important ingredient. Humor is also important.

Other healing rituals are those we use to give one another comfort when we are physically sick or emotionally stressed. For example, giving a back rub, listening without interrupting when the spouse is upset and just needs to vent, or just being silently present during a moment of physical or emotional pain. Sometimes, these healing rituals are created through difficult and honest conversations.

I remember when our children were very young, I would come home from work looking forward to relaxing and would be approached by Teri expecting me to take over the running of the house. I was tired, and she was too and we both wanted a break. It took some honest conversations for us to understand each other's needs and to create a ritual of transition. This is different from couple to couple. For example, a friend of ours, the mother of three, shared with us, "I have learned that when Paul gets home from his high-stress job, he needs a little time to transition, so we agreed that he needs about 20 minutes to wind-down. After about 20 minutes, he takes over and gives me a break. We had to figure out what works for us."

Reflection:

Examples of love rituals through which we forgive and help one another heal.

In reflecting on the presence of these love rituals in the life of your family, ask yourself: In our family how do we reconcile after a hurt? And, how do we comfort one another when one is sick or stressed out?

Read the sample list below and place a check mark by those rituals that remind you of what you already do in your home. Then, add any that you do that are not listed here. Finally, ask yourself: which of our love rituals could be improved, such as how we handle our disagreements?

Sample love rituals:

- An agreed-upon signal that says: "we have a problem and need to talk."
- During an argument that is spiraling out of control, a mutually agreed-upon signal that says "We need to take a break" to cool down.
- An expression of contrition: "Please forgive me. I'm sorry!"
- A hug, a handshake, a pat on the back, or a kiss to signal reconciliation. All of these says: we are OK, we are ready to put what happened behind us.
- Letting our spouse heal by venting without interruptions or advices. This is a way to show that we care when someone is upset and needs to vent about a pain originating outside the relationship.
- The act of metaphorically "biting one's tongue" when we disagree so that we can pay attention, listen, and hear what our child or spouse needs.
- Acts of caring for someone who is sick—being present to tend to their physical or emotional needs.
- A backrub, a massage, words of affirmation.
- A caress or a touch to express reassurance.

Any others?

3. **Rituals Through Which We Serve One Another for the Good of All**—These are rituals through which family members help one another, and through these the life of the family moves forward. Many such rituals are carried out by one person for the benefit of all. In a sense, the whole family is involved because everyone depends on certain individuals' contributions for the running of the home life. For example: cooking a meal, doing the laundry, washing the dishes,

guiding or correcting a child, paying the bills, spending time with a child doing schoolwork, and more, these are rituals of service. Each family has its own way of carrying on their life by performing the necessary tasks for the good of the whole. This includes ways in which family members contribute to the community.

One dimension of service, which applies to parents is the task of coaching their children's behaviors – discipline. All parents want their children to grow up as responsible adults, and therefore set expectations and rules to guide them, and they protect them by creating boundaries. This is a difficult parental task because as the children grow the expected behaviors change and at the same time the boundaries need to be expanded. Most parents are looking for a magic formula to accomplish this, and volumes have been written about this subject. You will not find that formula here, but more will be said in Chapter 6.

Reflection:
Examples of love rituals through which we serve one another.
In reflecting on the presence of these love rituals in the life of your family, ask yourself: How do I contribute to the life of my family? What do we do as a family to help those in our community who are in need?

Read the sample list below and place a check mark by those rituals that remind you of what you already do in your home today. Then, add any that you do that are not listed here. Finally, ask yourself: which of our love rituals in this category could be improved?

Sample love rituals:
- Cleaning the house
- Doing the laundry
- Taking care of the yard
- Making the beds
- Paying the bills

- Going to work
- Grocery shopping
- Cooking meals
- Supervising the children
- Keeping the cars in working order
- Carpooling the children to school or other activities
- Spending time with the children: homework, individual or group playtime.
- Donating food to the local food pantry.
- Helping with a community project.
- Volunteering to serve in ministries at the parish.

And many others.

In the Sacraments Christ Feeds our Love

Christ's love for the Church as expressed through the rituals of the seven sacraments is the model for loving in our homes. But Christ's love as expressed in the sacraments is not just our model for loving it is also the source of graces for us. Our participation in the sacraments of the Church gives us the grace we need to learn to love; it gives us the strength to actually carry out act of love in our family. In other words, the fire of love that warms our domestic church, our family, must be fed and sustained by the graces we receive in the sacraments. It is therefore important that we partake in the sacraments regularly, especially the Eucharist and Penance.

Through our participation in the sacraments Jesus feeds us and gives us the grace to be more welcoming and accepting of one another, more faithful, generous, forgiving, compassionate, and attentive to the needs of the people in our life. Christ's grace fuels the love of our family and help us perfect it, as St John writes: "Love one another, God abides in us and his love is perfected in us" (1 John 4:12).

The love rituals of the family, the domestic church, from a good morning kiss, to saying "I'm sorry," to cleaning the toilet, to caring for a sick child are all expressions of love that mirror the goodness of God's love, and teach your children what it means to be loved, and to love like Christ loves. In this home environment guided by faith your family will grow in faith and learn to love. Your home life will truly be an apprenticeship to loving.

Seven Daily Love Rituals for Couples

Because the relationship of husband and wife in a family is the heart of the domestic church, we need to do all that is possible to keep that bond strong. Therefore, I close this chapter with a list of seven key love rituals to strengthen your marriage. Do the following each day for a week, and you will feel closer to your spouse. Make these your daily habits, and you will have a strong marriage.

1. Say a prayer together. Keep it as simple as an "Our Father."
2. Say goodbye upon leaving and welcome each other home.
3. A six-second kiss (yes, just like in the movies). Dr. John Gottman, a noted researcher on marriage, says that six seconds is long enough to make you feel romantic.
4. Have a meal together.
5. When you disagree, bite your tongue, and listen to understand before you speak.
6. A gentle touch with the words, "I love you!"
7. Help your spouse with a chore. Make it a surprise.

The feelings that these rituals generate will strengthen your relationship; they will give you a taste of the goodness of God's love and will teach your children how to love.

Reflection:
- Which of the seven love rituals for couples do you do regularly?
- Which of the seven daily rituals is the easiest for you?
- Which of the seven daily rituals is most difficult for you?

Action:

Whether you are a co-parent or a single parent, you know that reflection and conversation are good, but without action, little progress is made in a family. Hopefully, this chapter has helped you realize that nurturing love and teaching love in your home are very important. What can you do to ensure that the love rituals you practice in your home contribute to teaching your children how to love? Start with one small action. Consider the suggestions below, and encourage other ideas from members of your family. Keep it easy and simple!

Write your plan here

_____

_____

I encourage you to track your family's journey as suggested on page 12 of the Introduction.

Suggestions:

1. Review your morning routines and rituals. Do you need to establish a ritual of greeting each other when you wake up? Or perhaps just doing better what you are already doing?
2. Review how you say goodbye to each other as each leaves home.
3. Review how you welcome each other back at the end of the day.
4. Review your habits about family meals and the conversations that go on during those meals.
5. Ensure that family meals are at the table and are not interrupted by TV watching, text messages, or phone calls.
6. Review your routines and rituals about retiring for the evening and going to bed for the night.
7. Review how you use such words as "Please," and "Thank you."
8. Does your family need to do better at saying "I'm sorry, please forgive me?"
9. Review your habits of how you deal with your differences.
10. Review with your spouse the seven daily rituals for couples.

Conversation Starters for Families

Below are topics for conversation with your children on the subject of loving one another in the family. You, as a parent or a grandparent, can bring these subjects up during informal chats at home, during car rides, or during meals. Use the questions below as conversation starters. Word them in a way that is appropriate for each child's age.

1. When was the last time someone was nice to you? How did you feel?
2. Through what words or actions do you express your affection toward your siblings or friends?
3. Is sitting down for a family meal something that you like? If so, what do you like about it? If "No," why not?
4. What do we talk about during a family meal? Which topics are of interest to you?
5. What is our routine before going to bed? What do you like about it, what do you not like?
6. What do you think about including in our bedtime routine a prayer, a blessing, and a "good night" kiss?
7. How do you feel when you come home and someone acknowledges you and welcomes you back?
8. How do you feel when someone who hurt you says to you, "I'm sorry, please forgive me"?
9. How can we help each other when someone is sick?
10. Explain to your children how they too can contribute to the running of the family and ask them: would you be willing to help your mom or dad in …(setting the table, doing the dishes, cleaning your room, mowing the lawn…)?

Conversation Starters for Parents or Groups

Notes for the group leader:

-Begin the meeting with the prayer to the Holy Family (end of Chapter 1).

-Start the conversation with a general question, such as: what did you find interesting and helpful in this chapter? What story touched you the most? What anecdotes or situations from your own life came to mind as you read the chapter?

-Continue the conversation by using the questions below.

-Close the meeting by asking participants to identify one thing they want to remember from the chapter or from the conversation that just took place.

1. What is the difference between an occasional act of kindness and a love ritual?
2. Which love ritual is most common in your home?
3. What is a love ritual that your family does well?
4. If you agree that your home is the place where your children learn how to love, describe what you do in your home that teaches them how to love.
5. What is one love ritual in your home you would like to improve?
6. What are some of the love rituals you learned in your childhood home?
7. Which love rituals do you want to pass on to your children because they are very important?
8. What are some of the love rituals of reconciliation and healing that you find helpful?
9. Which love rituals of service are most needed in your home, and who does them?
10. Of the seven daily rituals for couples, which one is the easiest for you, and which is the most difficult?

Prayer:

A Parent's Prayer, found at the end of Chapter 1, or the **Prayer to the Holy Family** found in the Appendix.

CHAPTER 5
HOME IS WHERE WE LEARN TO LIVE IN GOD'S TIME

Each Day is a Wonderful Gift from God

A few years ago, I traveled to Prague, the capital of the Czech Republic. I was there on business, but I also found the time to visit some of the popular tourist sites, among these the famous astronomical clock. This six-centuries-old clock is mounted on the tower of the town square. The face of the timepiece is very elaborate and colorful, and it shows not only the time of the day but also the position in the sky of the sun, the moon, and the signs of the zodiac. It is flanked by several statues, among them four mechanical ones that move each hour. They represent the four things to be avoided: vanity, greed, death, and lust. Above the face of the clock there are two small windows and above those there is a golden rooster.

On a snowy Saturday afternoon, I found myself standing with numerous spectators looking up at the tower and waiting for the hour to strike. Then, all of a sudden, I heard the ringing of a bell, the crowd quieted, and the mechanical figures started moving. I noticed that the bell ringer was the skeleton on the right side of the clock. The skeleton, the symbol of death, was calling everyone's attention to the passing of time. Death is coming! Some of the figures next to the skeleton were shaking their heads to say that they are not ready. Then two windows located above the face of the clock opened, and a procession of the 12 Apostles began. The Apostles remind us of our faith. At the end of the procession, the windows closed, and we heard the crow of the rooster located at the very top of the clock. The rooster represents life announcing the beginning of another hour. The hour struck; it was 3:00 pm.

At the end, as I stood with the other bystanders, still looking up, I was reminded that time is passing, our days on earth are numbered, and each hour and each day are a wonderful gift from God. Those moments of being transfixed on the symbolisms of the clock were a meditation on the gift of time.

The fact is that we live in God's time. He decides when we are born and counts our days until we return to him. The words of the psalmist remind us of this: "You knit me in my mother's womb; I praise you, because I am wonderfully made; in your book all were written down; my days were shaped, before one came to be" (Ps. 130:13-16)

All our days are written in God's book. At the end of our life, when we return to Him, He will ask us, "What did you do with the time I gave you? This reminds me of Jesus' parable of the talents in which the master gave his servants a certain number of talents, expecting them to be put to good use. When the master returned, he asked his servants to account for how they used their talents to profit him.

As we go through the struggles of daily life and the pursuit of our dreams, it is easy to forget that we are here to serve God during the time we are given. Time passes quickly, and we tend to take it for granted and even waste it. Often, we are not consciously aware of the passing of time. Have you ever been so engrossed in doing something that you did not realize how much time had passed? Time is our most precious commodity. The clock that counts our days is always running and we cannot stop it.

Reflection:

- When you read that your days are numbered, how do you feel?
- In what ways are you serving God during the time he has given you?
- Are you happy with the way you manage your time, especially time spent on the Internet and social media?
- Are you spending enough time being present to your spouse and your children?

A Lesson Learned

I spent one year after my high school in a novitiate, a place where young men discern their vocation to serve the Church as members of a religious order. I was considering membership in a missionary religious order. Each Wednesday, during the school year, we were given a day off from classroom learning. On that day, we worked on various projects or went on excursions in the mountains. The school was located in a valley in the Alps, in northern Italy. One day, we returned from one of our outings over one hour late. It was not the first time that we had been tardy, and the schoolmaster was very irritated by the incident. The next day, during an assembly, he reminded us of the importance of being aware of the passing of time and the need to be punctual in everything we do. He said that he had noticed that our tardiness was becoming a habit. Then added, "I know that all of you have watches to keep track of time. Obviously, your watches are broken, or you do not pay attention to them. So, please take off your watches and give them to me." We looked at each other and reluctantly took off our wristwatches, and one by one brought them to him. "From here on," he continued, "I want you to be on time without the need of a watch. Get in touch with the rhythms of nature. Look at the position of the sun in the sky, listen to your bodies, and listen to the bells on our school's tower to tell time. The bells chime every 15 minutes, and I expect you to be punctual." At the time, we did not have cell phones to tell us the time. The school master intended to teach us a lesson about the importance of time and the need to be aware of its passing. This exercise lasted about one month. The lesson was not appreciated by the student body, but much was learned from it.

We have limited time on this earth, and we are to use it wisely. In creating us, God gave us daylight and nigh-time, the phases of the moon, and the seasons. Based on these, we humans designed a calendar to help us organize our time: days, weeks, months, years so that we can keep track of the progress of our life's journey across time. We have come to value milestones, and we like to celebrate them: birthdays, anniversaries, graduations, job promotions, and other special events. Let's make these celebrations moments of gratitude toward God's providence, and opportunities for acknowledging the people in our life who have helped us along the way.

Reflection:
- Do you tend to be punctual or tardy?
- Have you ever had to tell time without the help of a watch or cell phone?
- Which milestones of your life have you celebrated this year?
- How does your family celebrate birthdays, anniversaries and graduations?

It's God's Time

In the Old Testament book of Ecclesiastes, the poet sings, "God has made everything appropriate to its time." There is a time to be born and a time to die; a time to weep and a time to laugh; a time to mourn and a time to dance. "There is an appointed time for everything" (Eccles. 3:1-12)

The psalmist tells us that God is everywhere, and we cannot escape his presence. We cannot hide from him; his providence guides us.

"From your presence where can I flee?
If I ascend to the heavens, you are there;

If I lie down in Sheol, there you are;
If I take the wings of dawn
and dwell beyond the sea,
Even there your hand guides me,
your right hand holds me fast" (Ps.139: 7-10)

When I was growing up, there was a phrase that seemed to be on everyone's lips when people spoke. My grandmother and my mother would say to a friend, "I will stop by on Tuesday to pick up some vegetables from you, God willing." "God willing" was a common expression that was part of the daily vocabulary in my family. Used often was also the Italian saying, "L'uomo propone, e Dio dispone" which loosely translated means "People make plans, and God decides" or "People propose, but God disposes." These expressions were often used out of habit and not necessarily out of deep faith, although faith was part of the culture. Regardless of the intent, the sayings conveyed a healthy attitude: our time and our life are a gift from God, he gives them to us at will.

Later, as I grew up and read the Bible, I found the source of such expressions of faith in the letter of James, chapter 4.

> Come now, you who say, 'Today or tomorrow we shall go into such-and-such a town, spend a year there doing business, and make a profit.' You have no idea what your life will be like tomorrow. You are a puff of smoke that appears briefly and then disappears. Instead, you should say, "If the Lord wills it, we shall live and do this or that." James 4:13-14

James' words help us keep our personal ventures into perspective. He writes that we are but a puff of smoke here today gone tomorrow. Thankfully, expressions of dependence on God have not disappeared from our language. Some time ago, I was meeting with a friend, and we were talking about something that had happened. I commented, "That was quite a coincidence." My friend corrected me,

"That was Providence," she said. On a different day, I visited my dentist's office for my regular teeth cleaning. The hygienist asked me, "Have there been any changes in your health since we last saw you?" I gladly replied, "No. Fortunately, I am in good health." The hygienist commented, "That is not a fortune. It is a blessing!" God's providence always surrounds us. We just need to recognize the blessings we receive.

Time spent in our home tending to the needs of the family is sacred because what we do in our home is sacred work. God's time is a mystery to us, but it is real. In our home, we shelter and nurture the most precious and sacred gift from God, the gift of life: ours and our children's. Within the bounds of our kitchen, bedrooms, and living rooms, we use our time to help one another grow, mature as human beings and give glory to God with our life. We help our children learn and acquire the interpersonal and intellectual skills that they need to grow up and take a role in society and in the Church. That requires an investment of time. Time spent tending the fires of love in our home is sacred time.

Reflection:
- In today's language, what expressions recognize the presence of God's providence in action?
- How would you propose to introduce in the daily language of your family faith-filled expressions of our belief that we live in God's time?

God's Time Has No Boundaries

A few years ago, I decided to clear out an old trunk in which we store items dear to us but that we seldom use. This was the trunk that held my belongings when I sailed from Italy to the USA, arriving in the port of New York in the fall of 1965. In this container, I found trays of slides for an old projector, copies of Life Magazine dating back to the 70s, many vinyl records, and other memorabilia. Among these was an old tape recorder with several reels of tape. I had not used this recorder in the past 30 years and did not know if it would still work.

In 1966, my family sent me that tape recorder to help me stay in touch with them. At the time, it was too expensive to communicate with my parents and siblings by phone, so every so often, I would record a short tape and then send it to them. The members of my family would pass the tape around for everyone to hear, and then they would prepare a recording for me. It was always a treat for me to receive one of these reels from Italy. Remembering fondly the content of these tapes, I went through the house searching for six large batteries to power the player. I was hoping the machine would still work.

When I turned it on, I heard, "Ciao Giovanni (my first name in Italian), I am Zio (Uncle) Luigi. I am here with your grandmother and your friends: the pastor of Castelletto, and his sister Caterina. There are also two nuns from the school and your sister, Sandra, who is running the tape recorder. With us is also the pastor's dog, Fido...."

The voice was not very clear, but the sound and the words transported me back to my youth. Memories of good times spent with each of those present flooded my mind. As each of them spoke to me via the tape recorder, it was like we were all sitting around the table together again.

The reality is that, except for my sister, all the people on the tape, including my uncle, my grandmother, the pastor, his sister, and the nuns have all passed away. Yet they were still alive to me at that very moment, thanks to the miracle of technology. Their voices were real, and the power of their words was moving me. The recording, which lasted 22 minutes, concluded with the distant sound of the church bells announcing the time to pray the Angelus. It was evening, and my Italian family and friends stood up and said the prayer: "The Angel of the Lord declared unto Mary. And she conceived of the Holy Spirit... Hail Mary full of grace..." as the tape ran out, they said,

"Please pray for us. We will pray for you." It was 8:30 pm, an evening in the summer of 1966.

God's time has no boundaries. We can pray for our loved ones after they are dead, and they can pray for us, as the Catechism reminds us, "Those who dwell in heaven… do not cease to intercede with the Father for us" (Catechism of the Catholic Church 956). This is possible because we are all part of what the Catholic Church calls the Communion of Saints, a grand family of believers who in life and death are united in Christ, and through him, we pray for one another. Pope Francis writes that our prayers for the deceased family members not only can help them but also can make their intercession for us more effective (AL 257).

I often pray for my parents and deceased family members when I attend Mass. After the Consecration, the priest recites a prayer for those who have passed. He says, "To our departed brothers and sisters and to all who were pleasing to you at their passing from this life, give kind admittance to your kingdom" (Eucharistic Prayer III). You too can pray for your deceased relatives and friends every time you attend Mass. Another occasion in which the Church encourages us to pray for our deceased relatives is the feast of All Souls Day, November 2.

Reflection:
- When and how do you remember your loved ones who have passed away?
- Do you pray for them? Do you ask them to pray for you?

Time in the Life of the Church

Although God's time has no boundaries, the Church, in her human dimension, sees the passing of days, weeks, and months not as a meaningless sequence of days, weeks, and months, but as the celebration of our redemption through a yearly cycle of seasons and feasts. Through these seasons, we celebrate events in the life of Christ, the feasts of Mary and the saints. At the epicenter of this redemptive cycle are Christ's death and Resurrection, which are commemorated in the spring, during Holy Week and Easter, and the Resurrection every Sunday, the Lord's Day.

Sundays – Celebrating the Lord's Day

In the Catholic Church's liturgical calendar Sundays have a prominent place because on that day, as members of the Body of Christ, we celebrate the Resurrection of Jesus. According the Scriptures, Jesus rose on the day after the Jewish Sabbath, our Sunday. This communal celebration is so important to our spiritual life that the Catholic Church, as a mother who cares for his children's souls, is telling all Catholics, that we have a serious obligation, to participate each week in the Sunday Eucharist.

"Participation in the communal celebration of the Sunday Eucharist is a testimony of belonging and of being faithful to Christ and to his Church." (Catechism of the Catholic Church 2182)

In today's post Covid pandemic times, it is important that we return to Sunday Mass in person. Private prayer, although important cannot replace our need for participation in the faith community's celebration of the Sunday Eucharist and the reception of Communion. During Covid we found it convenient and even beneficial to watch Mass on-line. That was often all that was available. Today, unless we are sick or have other serious reason, we need to return to Sunday Mass in person. As we return, let's remember what an important event this is in your life and in the life of your Catholic community. So, plan for it and dress appropriately for it. How we dress often speaks of the importance of what we do. It used to be that people wore their Sunday best to attend Sunday Mass. And, why not do so today?

In the Church's mind, the celebration of the Lord's Day

spans the whole day. In our tradition Sundays have been considered days of rest and relaxation. In today's world that runs 24/7, not everyone can spend Sunday at rest. Many people must work. We all have to do what we can, following as close as possible the guidance of the Church.

A leaflet published in 2010 by the United States Conference of Catholic Bishops lists examples of activities that are uplifting and appropriate for our Sunday celebration at home. Here are some.

- Share a family meal after Mass
- Spend time in fun activities with your family
- Go for a walk and give thanks to God for the beauty of nature.
- Spend time reading a spiritual book or Bible stories to your children
- Pray the Rosary
- Visit homebound parishioners
- Turn off your gadget and enjoy the silence.

Reflection:
- How does your family celebrate the Lord's Day?

Fridays – Days of Penance

Just as on Sundays we celebrate Christ's resurrection, which occurred on Easter Sunday, on Fridays we remember Christ's passion, which took place on Good Friday. On Fridays, throughout the year, Catholics are encouraged to abstain from meat or to do some sacrificial act, such as, giving up a favorite treat, or do something special for someone – corporal works of mercy. Through our penance we remember Jesus' sacrifice and join him in his redemptive suffering.

Reflection:
- What can you do on Fridays to remember Jesus's passion and death for our salvation?

The Liturgical Seasons

This cycle of sacred time is tracked with a liturgical calendar that is given to us by the Church to help us grow in our faith. Prominent on this calendar are the seasons of Advent, Christmas, Ordinary Time, Lent, Easter Triduum, Easter, and again Ordinary time. During these seasons, we accompany Christ on his journey among us. From his birth to his death and Resurrection, and Ascension to the Father.

The Advent Season marks the beginning of the liturgical calendar. Advent starts four Sundays before Christmas and is a time of waiting and spiritual preparation for Christ's second coming and the celebration of his birth, which we observe on December 25th. During Advent, the color of the vestments worn by the priest at Mass are purple, and rose on the third Sunday of Advent. Purple stands as a reminder to us of the need for penance and repentance as we wait for the second coming of the Lord. The color rose represents our joy that Christ is coming soon.

Catholic families celebrate Advent in their home with various traditional practices, such as the Advent wreath, the Jesse Tree, the Advent calendar, or reading passages from the Bible. Others build a nativity scene to remind themselves visibly of the events narrated in the Bible about the birth of Jesus. This last was the primary way that my family celebrated Advent when we were growing up. As children, we built what we, in Italy, called "il Presepio," an elaborate rendition of a landscape with hills, rivers, sheep, shepherds, and yes, also a stable with Mary and Joseph. This process took weeks, and while we played with the figurines, my parents retold the story of Jesus' birth, and we relived it in our imagination.

A friend shared with me: "In my home, during the Advent season, our parents would give each one of us children an envelope with pieces of paper straw. They told us that every time we were kind or helpful, we could place a piece of straw in the manger of the nativity scene. We wanted to make the manger for the Baby Jesus soft and comfortable, come Christmas day."

The Christmas Season celebrates the birth of Jesus, our savior, God incarnate. The Christmas season begins with the Mass on Christmas Eve. During the weeks that follow, we also celebrate the feast of The Holy Family, The Presentation of the Lord, The Epiphany, and The Baptism of the Lord, which marks the end of the Christmas season. The Church's color during Christmas time is white. White represents the joy of the Church for the gift of the Savior. On Christmas day, Catholic families that have assembled a nativity scene add the figurine of Baby Jesus to the manger. There are many other traditions, such as gift-giving and a variety of foods for the occasion.

Reflection:
- Growing up, how did your family celebrate the season of Advent and Christmas?
- Does your family practice any of the following traditions: Advent wreath, Jesse tree, nativity scene, Christmas tree, going to confession, Christmas angel, the Epiphany, and others?
- How does your family celebrate Christmas today?

Ordinary Time, Part 1, is the time between the end of the Christmas season and the start of Lent. During this time, through the Gospel readings, we walk along with Christ, like his disciples did, as he travels throughout Israel. We listen to his teachings, and we witness his miracles. Ordinary time is divided into two parts. The first part starts on the Monday after the feast of the Baptism of Jesus and ends the day before Ash Wednesday. The second part begins on the Monday after Pentecost and lasts until the evening before the First Sunday of Advent. During the season of Ordinary Time, the color of the vestments worn by the priest at Mass is green. Green represents life, hope, and anticipation.

The Lenten Season is a 40-day period of preparation for

the celebration of Easter. It is a period of penance, prayer, and almsgiving to ready ourselves to join Christ's passion on Good Friday and to celebrate his rising on Easter Sunday. The start date for Lent varies each year depending on the date of Easter, which is different according to the lunar calendar. Easter in the Catholic liturgical calendar is always the first Sunday after the first full moon of Spring. The color for Lent is purple to remind us that this is a time of penance and sacrifice, and the color rose, on the fourth Sunday of Lent, to express our joy for the upcoming celebration of Christ's passion and resurrection.

Reflecting on Lent, Pope Francis, on March 5, 2021, spoke to those gathered on St. Peter's Square for the Angelus, "I wish everyone a good journey in this Season of Lent. I recommend you fast, a fast that will not make you hungry: a fast from gossip and slander. This is a good fast."

Speaking of fasting, on Ash Wednesday and Good Friday, all Catholics are required to abstain from eating meat and to fast. Abstention from meat is also required every Friday during Lent for anyone older than 14. Fasting is not required of anyone younger than 18 and older than 59. When fasting, a person is allowed to eat one full meal and two smaller meals that together are less than a full meal.

Reflection:

- What does Lent mean to you? What memories do you have of Lent in your childhood?
- What practices are observed by your family during this time of prayer, penance, and almsgiving, such as fasting and abstinence, attending Ash Wednesday service, going to confession, donating to charities, and others?

The Easter Triduum is the shortest liturgical season: three days. It begins on Holy Thursday and closes the evening before Easter Sunday. As mentioned before, the rituals performed during these days commemorate pivotal events in the story of our redemption. On Holy

Thursday, we remember Christ's gift of the Eucharist during the Last Supper; on Good Friday, we relive Jesus' passion and death; on Holy Saturday, we meditate on his burial and wait for his rising on Easter Sunday. The Triduum ends after the Easter Vigil, on Holy Saturday evening. The colors displayed by the Church during this brief period of time are white on Holy Thursday and red on Good Friday. Red represents sacrifice.

The Easter Season begins at the end of the Easter Vigil and lasts for seven weeks (50 days), leading to the feast of Pentecost. This is the happiest time in the life of the Church. It is a time of joy because Christ has risen. Toward the end of the Easter Season, we celebrate the feast of Christ's Ascension into heaven. This is followed by the feast of Pentecost, in which we remember the descent of the Holy Spirit on the Apostles and the start of the mission of the Church. The color used by the Church to display her joy during this season is white.

Reflection:
- How did you observe Holy Week and Easter as a child?
- If you have attended the services during the Triduum, which liturgical ritual touched you the most?
- How does your family celebrate Easter? Do you celebrate with special traditions and foods?

Ordinary Time, Part 2, is the season that fills the rest of the year from the Monday after Pentecost to the evening before the first Sunday of Advent. As mentioned earlier, during this season, we read Gospel passages about Jesus' life, his miracles, and his teachings, and the history of our salvation as told in the Old Testament. Ordinary time is a time of hope and waiting, which is represented in the color green worn by the priest during the liturgical services.

The liturgical calendar guides Catholic families through the year with constant reminders of what we believe and of our obligation to honor and worship God. Among these reminders is the obligation of attending Mass on Sundays and other special days of obligation during the year. The Catholic Bishops in the United States have identified the following six feasts as days in which Catholics are to attend Mass: The Solemnity of Mary Mother of God, January 1ˢᵗ, The Ascension of Jesus (date changes), The Assumption of the Blessed Virgin Mary, August 15, Solemnity of All Saints, November 1ˢᵗ, Immaculate Conception of the Blessed Virgin Mary, December 8, and The Nativity of our Lord Jesus, December 25.

Interspersed throughout the year are feasts of the Blessed Virgin Mary, St. Joseph, the apostles and the saints. Each day in the Church's calendar is dedicated to celebrating the life of a saint to whom we turn for inspiration and intercession.

Just as the spiritual life of the Church revolves around the story of our salvation celebrated through the rituals of the liturgical seasons, so is the spiritual life of the family, the domestic church. To celebrate the liturgical seasons of the Church in your home is a faith enriching experience. This is what many Catholic families already do, and many wonderful traditions have been created and passed on from generation to generation that help us remember God's entrance into time and space to be with us and to save us—the Incarnation. Through these celebrations and with God's graces, we affirm our faith and strengthen it.

Reflection:
- Which of the seasons in the Church's calendar is your favorite, and why?
- Which feast of Mary is most familiar to you?
- What family tradition, inspired by the liturgical celebrations of the Church is most dear to you?

Celebrate Your Family's Spiritual Milestones
We read in the Catechism of the Catholic Church: "The Sacraments touch all the stages and all the important moments of

Christian life." #1210. During the liturgical seasons of the Church, families celebrate the reception of the sacraments - the spiritual milestones of the Catholic family: Baptisms, First Confessions, First Communions, Confirmations, Matrimonies, and for some families, priestly Ordination. There are also spiritual milestones for families whose member enter the religious life, such as the religious profession, the vow to observe the three Evangelical Counsels: Poverty, Chastity and Obedience.

Families prepare their members to receive some of these sacraments and they celebrate these events first of all with prayers and also with gifts, foods, and traditions often passed on from generation to generation. For example, some families use baptismal gowns warn by other family members at their baptism. Gifts are also given to encourage growth in the faith. When our oldest was baptized my brother gave her a golden necklace with a medal of Mary, which she still treasures. My wife, Teri has a rosary given to her by her uncle on the occasion of her Confirmation. She uses it every evening when we recite the Rosary in our home. At our wedding, our pastor gave us a large Bible, which we still use today, and consider our "family's Bible."

Celebrating your family's spiritual milestones is a way to honor and recognize the growth in faith of your family's members.

Reflection
- Do you remember the gifts you received for your First Communion and Confirmation? What were they?
- What traditions does your family have for celebrating the spiritual milestones of its members?
- If you do not have family traditions, about celebrating the spiritual milestones of your members, which ones would you like to start?

Action:

Hopefully, this chapter has helped you realize that time is a gift from God, and your home is the place where children learn that we live in God's time. What can you do today to remind your children that time is a gift from God and we are to use it wisely? Start with one small action. Consider the suggestions below, and encourage other ideas from members of your family. Keep it easy and simple!

Write your plan here:

_____

_____

I encourage you to track your family's journey as suggested on page 12 of the Introduction.

Suggestions:

1. Start using the phrase: "God willing…" when making plans.
2. Identify an upcoming feast of Mary or a saint which you want to celebrate with your family by attending Mass.
3. Decide which faith-inspired traditions you want to carry on in your family during Advent or Lent (whichever season comes next on your calendar).
4. Teach your children about the liturgical seasons and the colors of the priest's vestments at Mass.
5. Teach your children that time is a gift from God, and it is important to use it as we are supposed to and not to waste it. Teach them to be punctual.
6. For a week, make an effort to be punctual as a family.
7. Pray as a family for your deceased relatives and friends.

Conversation Starters for Families

Below are topics for conversation with your children on the subject of living in God's time. You, as a parent or a grandparent, can bring these subjects up during informal chats at home, during car rides, or during meals. Use the questions below as conversation starters. Word them in a way that is appropriate for each child's age.

1. Show your children a clock and tell them that the clock tracks the time that God is giving us each day.
2. Explain to your children the importance of using wisely the time given to us.
3. Each evening, ask your children, "What can we say and do to thank God for the time he has given us during this day?"
4. Ask your children what they hope to be doing tomorrow, and then explain that, God willing, those things may happen.
5. If appropriate, ask your children if they ever think about the people in your family who are deceased. Then explain that we should pray for them so that they will be in heaven as soon as possible to pray for us.
6. Talk with your children about Advent, Christmas, Lent, Easter, and other liturgical seasons and feasts and remind them of what they mean to the Christian community. Then explain how your family joins the Church in celebrating the Christian mysteries through your family traditions at different times of the year.
7. Share with your children your childhood memories of family traditions during Advent, Christmas, Lent, or Easter.
8. Point out to your children how all of these festivities revolve around what Jesus did for us.
9. Explain to your children why we go to Mass every weekend and Holy Days of Obligation.
10. If a member of your family is not Catholic, invite them to share how sacred time is celebrated in their faith tradition.

Conversation Starters for Parents or Groups

Notes for the group leader:

-Begin the meeting with the prayer to the Holy Family (end of Chapter 1).

-Start the conversation with a general question, such as: what did you find interesting and helpful in this chapter? What story touched you the most? What anecdotes or situations from your own life came to mind as you read the chapter?

-Continue the conversation by using the questions below.

-Close the meeting by asking participants to identify one thing they want to remember from the chapter or from the conversation that just took place.

1. When you read about your days being numbered, how do you feel?

2. How do you manage your time when using the Internet and social media?

3. What are some of life's milestones that your family celebrates, and how do you celebrate them?

4. What expressions in today's language recognize that God's providence is the ultimate arbiter of how things turn out?

5. When and how do you remember your loved ones who have passed?

6. How does your family celebrate the seasons of Advent and Christmas with the Church?

7. How does your family celebrate Lent, Triduum, and Easter?

8. Have you attended the church services during Holy Week (Holy Thursday, Good Friday, and Easter Vigil)? If so, what emotions have they evoked in you?

9. How could you celebrate birthdays and anniversaries in a way that expresses not only the joy for your achievements but also your gratitude to God for the time and opportunities given?

10. If a member of your group is not Catholic, invite them to share how sacred time is celebrated in their faith tradition.

Prayer:

A Parent's Prayer, found at the end of Chapter 1, or the Prayer to the Holy Family found in the Appendix.

CHAPTER 6

HOME IS A TRAINING CAMP FOR DISCIPLESHIP

Training Camp

When I first moved to the United States from Italy, I lived in Buffalo, NY, where I went to college and met a family that welcomed me into their home as one of their own. I visited them often and enjoyed the company of their five boys. Their home was my home away from home. What was interesting to me about this American family is how the parents, especially the father, chose to raise their sons. He wanted them to be athletes. Their house was like a gym. In the garage, they had a variety of fitness machines, treadmills, weightlifting benches, and many others. Everyone in the family was an avid fan of the Buffalo Bills. Football seemed to be all they talked about during their meals. They played the sport year-round in their yard, even in the snow. To me, coming from Italy, where American football was not known at the time, this was a novelty. The family's living room and the boys' bedroom were decorated with trophies earned by the father and the sons. Most of the trophies and medals were for victories in Greco-Roman wrestling matches. The family excelled, especially at this sport. I was often cajoled into wrestling one of the sons, and although I gave it my best, I had no chance of winning.

The sons grew up to be very good athletes. They went to

college on athletic scholarships. After I left Buffalo, I lost contact with the family, and I do not know if any of the young men pursued sports professionally. But, looking back at my experience during my years when I knew the family, I can say that this family's home life was truly a training camp for future athletes.

I believe that a Catholic family's home life needs to be a training camp for disciples of Jesus. A friend of mine, Parnell Donahue, M.D., a pediatrician with 40 years of experience and an author of parenting books, believes that the family passes on the Christian faith to their children by osmosis. Having lived in Wisconsin, he compares how Catholic families pass on the faith to how the Green Bay Packers fans pass on their Packers' enthusiasm to their children. Parents who are fans of the Packers dress up with the paraphernalia of the team, they talk about the games during meals and at family gatherings, and most of all, they attend or watch the games. At the stadium, they actively participate in chants that are intended to arouse the fans and players, and they wear the official headdress: the cheese-head. "That is a fervor that is contagious," says Dr. Donahue. Such needs to be our fervor for being on Christ's team.

Are we as enthused about our Catholic faith as sports fans are about their teams? We need to be. At our children's baptism, we accepted the responsibility to raise saints. The equipment and tools we use for this task are not physical, like in a gym or like the paraphernalia of a sport's fan. Our tools are the loving environment of our home, family's prayer, conversations about what we believe, reading the Bible, and the participation in the sacraments of the Church. In our role as parents, we are the first trainers and coaches of our children's faith on the path to discipleship, and there is nothing more effective than our personal example and guidance. As the adage goes: actions speak louder than words. Our goal is to lead our children to encounter Jesus and to know him through our example. This is expressed in the Catechism, "Parents have the first responsibility for the education of their children. They bear witness to this responsibility first by creating a home where tenderness, forgiveness, respect, fidelity, and disinterested service are the rule... Parents have a grave responsibility to give good example to their children" (Catechism of the Catholic Church 2223)

Reflection:

- In your opinion, what is the most important action parents can take to pass on the Christian faith to their children?

- How is your home a spiritual training camp for your children? How are you using the tools mentioned here: your personal example, family prayer, the loving environment of your home, the use of the Bible, and the participation in the sacraments?

The Power of Our Example

When I was in grade school, my father belonged to the Society of St. Vincent de Paul at our parish. Each year, during the weeks before Christmas, the Society distributed food baskets to the widowed in town. One day, my father asked me to accompany him to deliver a basket to an elderly lady who lived near us. As it was customary, we did not just drop the food basket at the door and immediately left. Instead, we accepted the invitation to stay and visit. She served us coffee, cookies, and chocolates. As a young boy, my interest was in the cookies and the chocolates. I did not pay much attention to the conversation. I remember that my father did not have to say very much. This was an opportunity for this lonely person to speak to someone, and she took full advantage. At one point, as we stood up to leave, my father asked the woman if she needed anything. She pointed toward her bathroom, complaining that she was having problems with her toilet; she said she had tried to fix it but was not successful. My father offered to check the toilet to see if he could be of help. The widow was glad for the offer. After a while, I heard my dad say, "I can fix your toilet, but I do not have the tools with me right now. If it is convenient for you, I will come back tomorrow and take care of it." He did return the next day and fixed the commode, and the widow was very pleased.

To me, as a child, what my father did was a clear lesson in neighborliness and charity. My father made time to care for one of our neighbors; he offered her food from his basket, listened to her needs, and fixed her toilet. That was all I could comprehend at the time, but that event has remained with me to this day as an example of discipleship. He did what Jesus would have done. My father did not have to explain anything to me. His example taught me to be aware of other people's needs—a lesson understood better years later.

The Catholic Church encourages us to practice the corporal works of mercy following the example of Jesus: feeding the hungry, giving drink to the thirsty, sheltering the homeless, clothing the naked, visiting the sick and the imprisoned, and burying the dead. I know a family that each year, on Thanksgiving Day, spends their holiday at the local homeless shelter. And so, parents, grandparents, aunts and uncles, and children all go to serve the Thanksgiving meal to people in need. Other families in my community collect canned goods and bring them to the parish for the local food pantry. Some couples serve as foster parents, and others adopt children who do not have a home; still others visit prisoners. Some lead programs for children with special needs, and others volunteer to serve as catechists. All of these charitable gestures motivated by our faith build memories in a child's mind about ways to follow the example of Jesus by sharing with others what we have been given.

Teaching our children to be disciples of Jesus is the first step in evangelization, and this is done by being and doing, more than talking; and most of all, it is done by personal example.

Reflection:

- What examples of Christian living did you witness in the actions of your parents, family members, or neighbors when you were growing up?

- How can you involve your children in your practice of the corporal works of mercy?

Passing on the Faith

Pope Francis, speaking to a group of parents on the occasion of the baptism of their children, said that faith is a gift that is passed on to the children by the example of their parents. "The important thing is to transmit the faith with your life of faith: that they see the love between spouses, that they see peace at home, that they see that Jesus is there" (1-13-2018). Our goal, as parents, is to help our children meet Jesus who is present in our life.

A parent's words in a moment of intimate conversation can have a great impact on the formation of a child's conscience. I remember a conversation I had with my mother when I was a child. One day, she told me while she was correcting me, "Don't think that you can hide from God. You can hide from me or your father, but you cannot hide from God. He sees you wherever you are, all the time. There is nothing that you can keep from him." Those words have become the voice of my conscience throughout my life. With time, as I matured, that watchful eye of God became for me my faithful companion and guide. The impact of my mother's words remains with me to this day.

Pope Francis' advice to parents on how to pass-on what we believe is very simple. He suggests that we repeat one short message to our children: "Jesus Christ loves you; he gave his life to save you; and now he is living at your side every day to enlighten, strengthen, and free you" (EG 164). Theologians call this formula the Kerygma. The Pope reminds us that this is the most fundamental message of our faith. Jesus loves you; he saved you, and he is with you right now, ready to help you. This simple proclamation of faith is a sermon that we parents can preach daily in our homes using a language appropriate for the age of each child.

For example, the first part of the message, "Jesus loves you" is one I have heard many parents proclaim when they pray with a child. Pope Francis paints a picture for us, "It is beautiful when mothers teach their children to blow a kiss to Jesus or to Our Lady. How much love there is in that! At that moment, the child's heart becomes a place of prayer" (AL 287).

The second part of the message: "Jesus gave his life to save us," is a more difficult concept, especially for the younger children, but it can easily be expressed by simply pointing to a crucifix. Explanations beyond that may not be necessary for a young child. If questions arise with older children, parents can respond in a way that helps the child understand Christ's role in our salvation, and his death and resurrection, without feeling overwhelmed. Emphasize that Jesus came to save us, to forgive us and to reconcile us with the Father. Through our Baptism he made us members of God's family.

The third part of the message is also simple: "Jesus is with you." This last part of the message is what has been emphasized throughout the chapters of this book. "Jesus is here standing by you" is a message that can be shared, especially when a child is afraid or upset and needs courage or confidence. "Jesus is with you, ready to help you. Just ask him."

We are the first educators of our children. In this role, we may encounter times when we do not have the answers to the questions our children are asking, especially as they enter their teen years. We need to remember that the Church has given us a wonderful tool to guide us: the Catechism of the Catholic Church. Every family needs to have a copy of the Catechism. This book provides a concise and clear summary of what the Church believes and teaches about God, the Church, our moral life, and prayer.

Reflection:

- In what ways do you see yourself telling your children: Jesus loves you; he saves us, he is with you?

Coaching your children

If your home is a training camp for discipleship, as this chapter proclaims, you as a parent are the coach. As parents we are tasked with forming our children's attitudes and behaviors. We want them to be disciples – discipline. The subject of discipline was touched on briefly in Chapter 3. Here I want to add a few more thoughts. Successful parents define for their children the behaviors that are expected, spell out the rules and set boundaries, then under their watchful eye they coach them to master certain skills. The effective coach watches each member of their team and gives them useful feedback. One of the key attitudes needed for successful parenting is caring presence. It is not helpful when parents set the rules and then ignore the children, and intervene only to punish a wrong behavior. Children and teens need the watchful eye of their guardians to guide them, admonish them, affirm them, encourage them and correct them when necessary. On the other hand, children also need the space to be themselves.

A useful educational model that applies to parenting and emphasizes the need for caring presence is one developed by St. John Bosco, called the Preventive System. It is called "preventive" because it avoids, as much as possible, the need for punishment. Punishment is the last resort, and corporal punishment is to be avoided. The system is based on reason, religion and a loving environment that supervises the child's behaviors and encourages what is good. The Preventive System is different from the laissez-fair style of parenting or the controlling and authoritarian style. St. John Bosco said that it is not enough to love our children, they must know that we love them. This is realized not in buying more toys and spoiling them but by showing our sincere concern for them – in being interested in what they are interested in.

The subject of specific parenting skills is one that goes beyond the scope of this book. If you are looking for helpful resources, I would encourage you to find articles and books inspired by St. John Bosco's approach to forming a child.

Your Home is Sacred Ground

That imperfect yet wholesome Catholic environment of my childhood home that I described in Chapter One did not make me a saint. Growing up, I was just a kid interested in soccer and playing with my friends. As a young boy, I looked at prayer and serving at Mass as something I had to do, like going to school or doing my chores. These religious activities were part of my daily routines, and often I did not want to do them. My faith was a very small seed planted within me at baptism, which needed a lot of nurturing and caring. But every day that I lived in my home, under the guidance and watchful eye of my parents, I inhaled the faith of my family, and with the passing of time, that seed began to grow. I came to realize that my life was part of something greater than myself, a plan designed by God, unknown to me, yet real. My parish priest once told me that I needed to nurture my relationship with God so that I could understand my vocation. That Catholic faith of my family helped me form habits that guided my prayer life and my behaviors to this day.

In retrospect, looking back at my childhood, I would say that my home was truly a spiritual training camp, a sacred space where my faith grew and was strengthened. The faith of my parents filled that space, and their example taught me how to live in the presence of God. As I matured, that faith directed me in charting my life's course and in creating a Christian home for my own family.

Your home is sacred ground in which your children's faith is planted and formed gradually, not through lectures but by example and with simple words at key moments of daily life. Some call these "teachable moments."

One evening, when I was about six years old, I was taking a stroll with my mother around our neighborhood. We came upon a wooded area where a large flock of birds was roosting. Their loud chirping caught my attention, and I asked my mom why they were so loud. She responded, "The noise you hear is the song of the birds reciting their night prayers like we do." That was a teachable moment. The lesson I learned was all creatures honor God. I thought to myself: "If the birds pray, I must also pray."

Years ago, when our youngest was in Junior High, one day, she came home from school and reminded Teri that she had invited one of her friends to the house. We live in Tennessee, and Catholics here are a small minority. Her friend was not Catholic. This conversation took place in the kitchen where, on the island, Teri was keeping a candle, some flowers, and a picture of Mary that I had purchased for her in Moscow. Our family was in the habit of lighting a candle in front of Mary for her intercession whenever someone asked us to pray for them. Pointing to the island and to the candle, our daughter said, "Can you remove this? My friend is not Catholic, and she will not understand." This interaction prompted a very important conversation about our faith, about who we are as a Catholic family, and what we tell people about what we believe. Teri did not move our little shrine.

Reflection:
- How has your view of life been shaped by the home environment you grew up in?
- What are some of your memories of faith practice in your childhood home?
- If strangers came to visit you at home today, how would they know that your family is Catholic? What would they see? What would they hear?

"It Takes a Village"

"It takes a village to raise a child" is said to be an African proverb that recognizes a parent's need for the support of their community.

A few years ago, I read a commentary by a British nanny who had served families in the United States for some time. Her advice to parents was to remember that they are part of a village and to let others help them. She wrote, "It used to be that bus drivers, teachers, shopkeepers, and other parents had carte blanche to correct an unruly child. They would act as the mum and dad's eyes and ears when their children were out of sight, and everyone worked towards the same shared interest: raising proper boys and girls. This village once offered support. Now, when someone who is not the child's parent dares to correct him, the mum and dad get upset."

The former nanny continues, "If a child is having a tantrum in public, all eyes turn on the mum disapprovingly. Instead, she should be supported: Hey, good work–I know setting limits is hard."

One Sunday morning, Teri was standing in line at the check-out counter at the local Walgreens store, and there was a family ahead of her. All the members of the family were dressed up, so she assumed they had just returned from church. It appeared that the son, a little boy, had stolen a small item, and the mother was not leaving until he returned it and apologized to the clerk. The child was refusing, and the line of customers at the check-out counter was growing longer. The mother turned toward Teri and the long line with a look that said, "I'm sorry!". After a short stand-off, the child realized they weren't leaving until he apologized. So, he returned the object that he had taken and said: "I'm sorry!"

As Teri watched the drama unfold, she thought about Pope Francis and wondered what he would do if he were standing there, witnessing this moment. So, as the family left the store, she followed them. Once outside, empathizing with the mom, she patted her on the back and said, "Good job, Mom!"

Pope Francis does recognize that we are a "village," and we need one another's to help raise our next generation. In a meeting with educators (9-6-2014), he lamented the fact that we have lost the sense of common responsibility to help one another's children, especially when parents and teachers are not on the same page. He said, "We must recompose the village to educate the child."

I remember an incident that happened to me when I was about eight years old. One day, my younger brother and I found one cigarette and promptly decided to smoke it. We left the house and went to the remotest part of our yard, out of my family's sight, and started smoking. We did not realize that our neighbor had full view of what we were doing. The neighbor lady came to the fence and said to us, "What are you boys doing?" Of course, she knew what we were doing. Feeling embarrassed for having been caught, we did not respond. She continued, "Please stop smoking right now and throw away the cigarette. Otherwise, I will tell your mother." The lady was a good neighbor! Her threat got our attention, and we complied. She did not talk to our mother, but the thought that she might remained a warning to us. Neighbors can be the best allies of parents.

We are all part of one human village and we need to look out for one another. We are all called to be good neighbors; to offer support and to pay special attention to the families in our neighborhood that are suffering: because of sickness, of financial difficulties, or relationship problems. Among these are the single parent families. These often feel excluded in a Church that rightly promotes intact families. Reach out to single parent families in your neighborhood to help them feel connected and give them a sense of belonging in your parish community. Their children need love, just as much as your children do. Share with them the love of your family.

Reflection:
- As a child, have you ever had a neighbor correct you?
- Who is your village, and in what ways is it helping you raise your children?
- Do you know the single parents in your neighborhood? What can you do to offer them your support?

Godparents and Grandparents

The members of the family's village who are nearest to the parents are the extended family. Prominent among these are grandparents and godparents. The Catholic Church, in her wisdom, has for centuries asked parents to provide their children a godfather or a godmother. In baptism, the role of the godparent is to present the infant for baptism along with the parents. Then their role during the life of the newly baptized child is to assist the parents in carrying out their Christian responsibilities of passing on the faith. Their role is also to lead a Christian life as models of Christian behavior to their godchild.

Grandparents are important members of every family's village. We are blessed when we have them close to us so that our children can learn from them and even be spoiled a little by them. Pope Francis commented during one of his Wednesday General Audiences, "Many of us learned how to whisper our first prayers on our parents' or grandparents' laps" (4-14-2021).

My grandfather, my mother's father, was also my godfather. He and I became very close during my growing-up years. From the age of two to the time I went to first grade, I spent many hours each day with him. When he went out to run errands, I would accompany him, and he would enjoy my company. As we walked the streets of our town, I would pepper him with questions, "What is that?" "Why do they do that?" He always had an answer for me. He was a religious man but would not talk about religion. For example, whenever we would pass in front of a church, and there were many in my Italian hometown, he would lift his hat out of reverence for the Eucharist in that tabernacle. On Sunday afternoons, he would take me with him to our parish church for the recitation of the vespers and benediction with the Blessed Sacrament. On occasion, he also introduced me to life's mysteries. One day during our walk about town, we came upon a funeral procession. It was the first one I had ever seen, and I did not know what it was. We stopped, and my grandfather removed his hat out of respect. So, I asked him what this was. Apparently, I did not understand what he said. The casket was on a carriage drawn by horses all decked out in black. Behind the carriage was a crowd of people praying the rosary. What caught my attention was the posture of one woman who was walking right behind the carriage. She was crying and was flanked by two men who seemed to be holding her up. In my young mind, I thought that the person crying was the one to be buried. That left me puzzled and concerned. So, I asked my grandfather, "When is the person crying going to die? And when will she be placed in the casket?" So, my grandfather gently and patiently re-explained the funeral to me. He reassured me that the lady crying was not the person to be buried.

Grandparents are teachers, mentors, surrogate parents, playmates, and friends and can have an important role in the religious formation of their grandchildren. It is unfortunate that today millions of people are long-distance grandparents. In a radio interview, before becoming pope (2012), Pope Francis said about his grandmother Rosa, "It was my grandmother who taught me to pray. She left a deep spiritual imprint on me and used to tell me stories about the saints."

My grandmother, Margherita, was the same for me. She was the one in our family who spoke openly about our faith and the need to pray. She would invite us to pray with her. There were days when she would wake me up at 5:30 in the morning to go with her to the 6:30 Mass, where she encouraged me to serve.

At times, grandparents have to stand in for the parents. According to an article published by US News, August 4, 2020, 2% of U.S. children (2.9 million) are raised by their grandparents. That is a heavy responsibility and burden to carry, after having lived a full life and raised their own family. In 2021, Pope Francis, wanting to recognize the contribution of grandparents, established a World Day for Grandparents to be celebrated by the Catholic Church each year on the fourth Sunday of July. He said, "They remind us that old age is a gift, and that grandparents are the ring linking generations, to transmit to young people the experience of life and faith."

Reflection:

- What are some of the memories of your godparents and grandparents?
- What is one valuable lesson you learned from your grandparents or godparents?

The Parish Community

The next group of people in a Catholic family's village are the neighbors and the members of their parish community and Catholic school. The family in Buffalo, NY, that was raising their sons to be athletes, succeeded in sending them to college on athletic scholarships because they had the support of others in their community. The parents' role was to help their sons enjoy sports and develop an interest in them. They encouraged the sons to pursue their athletic dreams. But those efforts alone would not have made their sons college-bound athletes. The boys succeeded because they were supported by a village made up of community organizations and schools that provided them with good teachers and coaches and opportunities to compete. They were also helped by relatives, friends, and neighbors who showed up to cheer them on at competitions.

No family lives in isolation. As parents, we need to realize that our children's religious faith and moral conscience will be formed not just by us but also by others who do not live under our roof: the friends they associate with, the teachers who guide them, and the electronic media they consume. Therefore, it is our obligation as parents to become active in a parish, a faith community that believes and lives the values we want to pass on to our children. What we teach and practice at home regarding our religious faith needs to be re-affirmed by our community. As the fans of any sports team become more fervent by attending games and spending time with other fans, our faith becomes more fervent through our participation in the sacraments, and spending time with members of our extended spiritual family.

Teri and I relocated to different cities five times during our marriage. For us, regardless of where we lived, we found an extended family in our Catholic parish. When relocating, one of the first decisions we made was to register at the local parish. That community became an extension of our family, not just because we were registered members but also because we became involved in the life of the community. We did so by attending Mass regularly, joining parish organizations, volunteering to be catechists, sending our children to the religious education program or to the Catholic schools where they were available, and to youth ministry activities. We found the support of our parishes to be very valuable to our family.

The educational resources that the parish community offers are very beneficial to the spiritual and moral development of your children. I recently read an article that reminded me of the positive influence of the parish on our children. There was a 10-year-old boy in Spain who was preparing to receive his First Communion. As the date approached, family members and relatives gave him gifts. One relative gave him an envelope with cash and said, "Use it to buy whatever you want." His parents thought he would buy a video game. The next morning, his mother pressed him, "What are you going to do with the money you received?" The child replied, "I am going to give it to the parish. At the parish, they teach me to help people in need. With the money, they will be able to help someone." Caring for the poor is what he had learned from his family, and it was reinforced by the religious training he received at the parish (Aleteia 24th 6-12-21).

As parents, we do not have control over what our children will do with their lives. Our duty is not to plan their lives but to provide a home environment during the formative years that nurtures their budding faith and prepares them for the challenges of life, and then let them go. From that point on, we can only pray that they will practice what we taught them, grow in their faith and be responsible citizens.

Reflection:
- Who were the people who influenced your spiritual and moral development the most?

- How are you active in your parish today?

Your Love and Your Faith Will Radiate from your Home

In the Old Testament, the prophet Ezekiel writes about a vision he had (Ezek. 47). He saw water flowing out of the doors of the temple into the surrounding lands and cities, and wherever that water reached, life flourished.

I believe that the same happens in our families. Love is at the center of our home, a force that keeps us together and gives life to our family. Like the water in Ezekiel's vision, our loving actions and words bring a touch of God's goodness to the people we meet beyond the boundaries of our home. The loving words and actions learned in our family help us carry the good news of the Gospel wherever we go.

Pope Paul VI wrote:

The family, like the Church, ought to be a place where the Gospel is transmitted and from which the Gospel radiates. In a family which is conscious of this mission, all the members evangelize and are evangelized. The parents not only communicate the Gospel to their children, but from their children they can themselves receive the same Gospel as deeply lived by them. And such a family becomes the evangelizer of many other families, and of the neighborhood of which it forms part. (EN 71)

Action:

      Hopefully, this chapter has helped you realize that your home life is very important to the Church, and it reminded you that when you had your children baptized, you agree to train them in the practice of your faith. What can you do today to renew your commitment to carry on that responsibility? Start with one small action. Consider the suggestions below, and encourage other ideas from members of your family. Keep it easy and simple!

Write your plan here:

_____

_____

I encourage you to track your family's journey as suggested on page 12 of the Introduction.

Suggestions:

1. As a family, identify two people who contributed the most to your Christian formation and send them a thank you note.
2. Tell your relatives and neighbors that if they see your children doing something they think is harmful, to please correct them and to tell you.
3. Celebrate Grandparents' Day, the fourth Sunday of July.
4. Tell your children who their godparents are, and encourage them to send them a note.
5. Identify something that you can do to be more active in your parish.
6. Purchase a copy of the Catechism of the Catholic Church.
7. Consider sending your children to a Catholic school or to a Religious Education Program.
8. If one of the parents is not Catholic, have a conversation about raising the children Catholic, and the support the Catholic parents would like to have in order to do so.

Conversation Starters for Families

Below are topics for conversation with your children on the subject of what it means to be a follower of Jesus. You, as a parent or a grandparent, can bring these subjects up during informal chats at home, during car rides, or during meals. Use the questions below as conversation starters. Word them in a way that is appropriate for each child's age.

1. Ask your children: "Who are the people in your life that you admire and listen to the most?"
2. "What do the people you admire do or say that you like?"
3. "What do you know about Jesus?"
4. "How do you love Jesus? How does he love you?"
5. "Jesus came on earth to save you. What does this mean to you?"
6. Jesus is right by you during our day—"When do you need his help the most?"
7. "Do you know who your godparents are? Let's say a prayer for them or write a note to them."
8. "How do you think Jesus wants you to love your brothers and sisters? What would he want you to do or avoid?"
9. As followers of Jesus, we love God and love everyone. "What have you done lately to help someone else?"
10. "What have you learned recently at Mass, at your Religious Education program, or at your Catholic school about following Jesus' example?"

Conversation Starters for Parents or Groups

Notes for the group leader:
-Begin the meeting with the prayer to the Holy Family (end of Chapter 1).
-Start the conversation with a general question, such as: what did you find interesting and helpful in this chapter? What story touched you the most? What anecdotes or situations from your own life came to mind as you read the chapter?
-Continue the conversation by using the questions below.
-Close the meeting by asking participants to identify one thing they want to remember from the chapter or from the conversation that just took place.

1. How is your home a spiritual training camp for your children?
2. What is the most important thing a parent can do to pass on the faith to their children?
3. How would you go about conveying to your children the basic Christian message suggested by the Pope: Jesus loves you; he gave his life to save you, now he is living next to you?
4. Who is your village?
5. In what ways is your village helping you raise your children?
6. What did you learn from your grandparents or godparents?
7. How do you involve your children's godparents and grandparents in their life?
8. Who are the people who influenced your spiritual and moral development the most, and how?
9. How are you active in your parish community?
10. If you are not Catholic, how do you feel about your children being raised Catholic? What support do you give to the Catholic parent?

Prayer:

A Parent's Prayer, found at the end of Chapter 1, or the **Prayer to the Holy Family** found in the Appendix.

CONCLUSION

The Role of the Parent

I am closing this book with the words of Pope Francis about the role of parents. Let these be your guide:

"Parents always influence the moral development of their children, for better or for worse. It follows that they should take up this essential role and carry it out consciously, enthusiastically, reasonably and appropriately" (AL 259).

"The important thing is to transmit the faith with your life of faith - by example" (1-13-2019).

"Parents need to consider what they want their children to be exposed to, and this necessarily means being concerned about who is providing their entertainment, who is entering their rooms through television and electronic devices, and with whom they are spending their free time. Only if we devote time to our children, speaking of important things with simplicity and concern, and finding healthy ways for them to spend their time, will we be able to shield them from harm. Vigilance is always necessary and neglect is never beneficial" (AL 260).

These are truly words of wisdom. They challenge me to an examination of conscience. Take up the leadership role in your family. Teach your children how to pray and pray with them and for them. Lead them, and they will follow you.

God will bless you and your children.

Reflection:

- What is the spiritual legacy that you want to leave to your children?

APPENDIX

Basic Catholic Prayers

The Sign of the Cross
In the name of the Father,
and of the Son,
and of the Holy Spirit.
Amen.

The Our Father
Our Father, who art in heaven,
hallowed be thy name;
thy kingdom come;
thy will be done on earth as it is in heaven.
Give us this day our daily bread;
and forgive us our trespasses
as we forgive those who trespass against us;
and lead us not into temptation,
but deliver us from evil.
Amen.

The Hail Mary
Hail Mary, full of grace, the Lord is with thee;
blessed art thou amongst women,
and blessed is the fruit of thy womb, Jesus.
Holy Mary, Mother of God,
pray for us sinners
now and at the hour of our death.
Amen.

The Glory Be

Glory be to the Father, and to the Son, and the Holy Spirit;
as it was in the beginning, is now, and ever shall be,
world without end.
Amen.

The Morning Offering

O Jesus, through the Immaculate Heart of Mary,
I offer you my prayers, works, joys, and sufferings of this day
for all the intentions of your Sacred Heart,
in union with the Holy Sacrifice of the Mass throughout the world,
for the salvation of souls, the reparation of sins, the reunion of all
Christians,
and in particular for the intentions of the Holy Father this month.
Amen.

Prayer to the Guardian Angel

Angel of God,
my Guardian dear,
to whom God's love commits me here,
ever this day be at my side,
to light and guard,
to rule and guide.
Amen.

Grace Before Meals

Bless us, O Lord,
and these Thy gifts
which we are about to receive
from Thy bounty,
through Christ our Lord.
Amen.

Act of Contrition

O my God, I am heartily sorry for having offended you,
and I detest all my sins because of your just punishment,
but most of all because they offend you, my God,
who are all good and deserving of all my love.
I firmly resolve with the help of your grace
to sin no more and to avoid the near occasion of sin.
Amen.

Prayer to St. Joseph

Hail, Guardian of the Redeemer,
Spouse of the Blessed Virgin Mary.
To you God entrusted his only Son;
in you Mary placed her trust;
with you Christ became man.
Blessed Joseph, to us too,
show yourself a father
and guide us in the path of life.
Obtain for us grace, mercy, and courage,
and defend us from every evil.
Amen.

Prayer to Saint Michael the Archangel

St. Michael the Archangel,

defend us in battle.

Be our defense against the wickedness
and snares of the Devil.

May God rebuke him, we humbly pray,
and do you, O Prince of the heavenly hosts,
by the power of God,
thrust into hell Satan, and all the evil spirits,
who prowl about the world seeking the ruin of souls.
Amen.

Family Blessing at Bedtime

May almighty God bless you
in the name of the Father,
and of the Son,
and of the Holy Spirit,
with life everlasting.
Amen.

Memorare

Remember, O most gracious Virgin Mary,
that never was it known
that anyone who fled to thy protection.
implored thy help,
or sought thine intercession was left unaided.
Inspired by this confidence,
we fly unto thee, O Virgin of Virgins our mother;
to thee do we come, before thee we stand,
sinful and sorrowful;
O Mother of the Word Incarnate,
despise not our petitions,
but in thy mercy hear and answer us,
Amen.

Prayer to the Holy Family

Jesus, Mary and Joseph,
in you we contemplate
the splendor of true love,
to you we turn with trust.

Holy Family of Nazareth,
grant that our families too
may be places of communion and prayer,
authentic schools of the Gospel
and small domestic churches.

Holy Family of Nazareth,
may families never again
experience violence, rejection and division:
may all who have been hurt or scandalized
find ready comfort and healing.

Holy Family of Nazareth,
make us once more mindful
of the sacredness and inviolability of the family,
and its beauty in God's plan.

Jesus, Mary and Joseph,
graciously hear our prayer.

Amen.

(Pope Francis, 2016, The Joy of Love)

AUTHOR

John Bosio, MA

Married 50 years, John and his wife, Teri, live in Mount Juliet, TN. They are parents of two daughters. John has led religious education programs and marriage enrichment at the parish and diocesan level for many years. He has a master's degree in theology and a master's degree in counseling. Together with his wife Teri, he served the Archdiocese of Kansas City in Ks as Family Life Coordinators. For 10 years, he supported three parishes in Kansas as a marriage and family therapist. From 1987 to 2011, he worked for two large corporations (Cummings Engine Co. and Caterpillar Inc) as an International Human Resources Manager.

While working in the corporate world, John continued his interest in marriage and family life. In 2008 published his first book *Happy Together, the Catholic Blueprint for a Loving Marriage,* followed by *Blessed is Marriage, a Guide to the Beatitudes for Catholic Couples,* in 2010, and in 2014 *Joined by Grace,* a marriage preparation program that he co-authored with his wife, Teri for Ave Maria Press. In 2019 they published *Six Jars of Love, Loving Attitudes to Help Married Couples Reconnect.*

At the same time, together with his wife, John developed three marriage enrichment programs widely used in parishes across the USA and in other English-speaking countries: *SIX DATES for Catholic Couples, The Beatitudes,* and *The Virtues.* For the past 12 years, John has contributed a monthly column on marriage to several diocesan publications.

Websites: www.happy-together.net and www.the-virtues.net

Books by the Author

Happy Together, The Catholic Blueprint for a Loving Marriage, Twenty Third Publications, 2008

Blessed is Marriage, A Guide to the Beatitudes for Catholic Couples, Twenty Third Publications, 2012

Why Get Married in the Church? The Lifelong blessings of a Catholic wedding, Twenty Third Publications, 2013

Joined by Grace, Preparing for the Sacramental Journey of Marriage, Ave Maria Press, 2016 – together with Teri Bosio

Joined by Grace, a Catholic Prayer Book for Engaged and Newly Married Couples, Ave Maria Press, 2017 – together with Teri Bosio

Six Jars of Love, Loving Attitudes to Help Married Couples Reconnect, Twenty Third Publications, 2019 – together with Teri Bosio

Video Programs

SIX DATES for Catholic Couples, growing your marriage guided by your Catholic faith, six videos, 2010

The Beatitudes, a Couple's Pat to Greater Joy, six videos, 2012

The Virtues, A Program for Couples, four videos, 2016 – available free at: www.the-virtues.net

Learn about these at: www.happy-together.net